Gabriel Ngwe

# Why Is Agricultural Trade Liberalization at a Stalemate?

Multilateral Negotiations between the United States, the European Community, and the G20 (2001-2006)

Gabriel Ngwe

# WHY IS AGRICULTURAL TRADE LIBERALIZATION AT A STALEMATE?

Multilateral Negotiations between the United States, the European Community, and the G20 (2001-2006)

*ibidem*-Verlag
Stuttgart

**Bibliografische Information der Deutschen Nationalbibliothek**
Die Deutsche Nationalbibliothek verzeichnet diese Publikation in der Deutschen Nationalbibliografie; detaillierte bibliografische Daten sind im Internet über http://dnb.d-nb.de abrufbar.

**Bibliographic information published by the Deutsche Nationalbibliothek**
Die Deutsche Nationalbibliothek lists this publication in the Deutsche Nationalbibliografie; detailed bibliographic data are available in the Internet at http://dnb.d-nb.de.

Cover picture: © bikemen / PIXELIO

∞

Gedruckt auf alterungsbeständigem, säurefreien Papier
Printed on acid-free paper

ISBN-10: 3-89821-860-0

ISBN-13: 978-3-89821-860-3



Printed in Germany

To my uncle Djagui Mbondo,
With gratitude

## CONTENTS

## Preface

This book was first submitted as a MA thesis at Jacobs University. The study emerged from a frustration that has arisen from my efforts to understand why trans-border trade in agricultural goods was characterized by different preferential trading agreements, while the manufacturing sector was substantially liberalized on a multilateral basis. The literature I reviewed in this regard did not appease my intellectual thirst. I was confronted with a great number of books that more or less described the 'messiness' of agricultural trade without exploring in the first place where this state of affairs came from. My question, therefore, why trans-border trade in agricultural goods was not subject to the kind of multilateral rules that govern international trade in manufacturing products, remained unanswered. As the ninth round of GATT negotiations (so-called Doha Round) came to a sudden halt in July 2006, I decided to grasp the opportunity and tackle the question of agricultural trade negotiations. While I was still indecisive whether I could explore this issue, Professor Welf Werner swept away my fears and comforted me with the idea that, indeed, it was possible to ask a 'why-question' as long as negotiations were stalled. From that very moment, I committed myself to study the stalemate in agricultural trade liberalization. However, this endeavour would not have materialized without the support of many persons, to whom I would like to express my sincere gratitude.

This work would not have taken the present form without the insightful comments of my supervisors and chairs of the MA program. My special gratitude goes first to both my supervisors, Professor Welf Werner and Professor Georg Ress. I am indebted to Professor Werner on the one hand because he constantly reminded me to read the most relevant journal articles on the subject, what turned out to be very helpful. I thank him for his readiness to discuss some controversial parts of the work with me and his insightful critiques in the process of writing the thesis. On the other hand, I am thankful to Professor Ress for his readiness to clarify some legal aspects of trade liberalization to me. As his student assistant in the seminar 'international trade law' at the time of writing the thesis, I got the opportunity to discuss some legal aspects of trade law with the other class mates. I owe a lot to Professor Peter Mayer and Professor Philipp Genschel, as chairs of the MA program 'International Relations' at the Jacobs University, for their comments and critiques to my first drafts. I do not forget all the other class-mates who participated in the colloquia. I particularly thank Prince Bona and Sennait Negash for having proof-read the final drafts of this study, and Kai Fink for helping to draw the figures.

Finally, I owe a large debt of gratitude to my family, Sylvie and Melanie Kinyock, living thousand of miles away from me, but with the conviction that 'every thing' will get better. I am above all grateful to my uncle Djagui Mbondo for his unstinting generosity, but also for being more than a father, to whom this book is dedicated. I do not forget my babies Ingrid and Jordan, my friends Dieter Ley, Flore Baleba, Gabriel Adzessa and all the rest.

It should be noted, however, that I alone bear full responsibility for the shortcomings of this book.

Bremen, November 2007

Gabriel Ngwe

## List of Acronyms

| | |
|---|---|
| AAA | Agriculture Adjustment Act |
| ACP | African, Caribbean, and Pacific group of countries |
| AoA | Agreement on Agriculture |
| CAP | Common Agricultural Policy |
| CCC | Commodity Credit Corporation |
| EC | European Community |
| IMF | International Monetary Fund |
| IATP | Institute for Agricultural and Trade Policy |
| ICAC | International Cotton Advisory Committee |
| GATT | General Agreement on Tariffs and Trade |
| GDP | Gross Domestic Product |
| G77 | Group of Seventy-Seven, composed of the developing countries members |

| | |
|---|---|
| G20 | Group of Twenty developing countries and more that joined together at the Cancún Ministerial Conference in 2003 to push for agricultural trade liberalization |
| G90 | A coalition of Least Developed Countries; the African, Caribbean, and Pacific Group; and the African Union |
| LDC | Least Developed Countries |
| OECD | Organization for Economic Cooperation and Development |
| TRQ | Tariff-Rate-Quota |
| USA | United States of America |
| USDA | United States Department of Agriculture |
| USTR | United States Trade Representative |
| WACIP | West Africa Cotton Improvement Programme |
| WTO | World Trade Organization |

# 1. Introduction

On July 2006, the already five-year-old Doha Round[1] of global trade talks came to a sudden halt. This study inquires about the causes of this stalemate in respect to agricultural trade negotiations between the United States (USA), the European Community (EC), and the G20. Multilateral negotiations to liberalize agricultural trade have always been a big challenge to the international trading system, as this was the case during the Dillon, the Kennedy, the Tokyo[2], and the Uruguay Rounds.[3] It was not until the Dillon Round that agriculture appeared on the agenda of multilateral trade negotiations.[4] However, little progress was made in this regard and "agriculture emerged as it entered, the most highly protected sector in national economies, the most undisciplined area of international commerce, and the cause of some of the most dangerous frictions in international economic relations".[5] Indeed, if agriculture is such a highly protected sector that leads to dangerous frictions in international economic relations, what could explain such state of affairs? Why should an activity that represents only about 13

---

[1] The Doha Round, also called the Doha Development Agenda, or the Millennium Round, is the follow-up of a reform process that started during the Uruguay Round. The Doha Round formally started on 1 January 2002 and was expected to be concluded on 31 December 2005, see Winham, in Ravenhill (2005: 112). The agricultural reform package of the Round is codified in the Agreement on Agriculture (AoA), in force since 1995.

[2] The Dillon Round (1960-61) was the fifth round of trade negotiations under the General Agreement on Tariffs and Trade (GATT). It concerned mainly the reduction of tariffs on manufactured goods and included 26 participants. The Kennedy Round (1964-1967) extended negotiations on anti-dumping measures and included 62 participants, and the Tokyo Round (1973-1979) further expanded the scope of negotiations which included non-tariff measures, the 'framework' agreements, known as the Tokyo Round codes, into the agenda; 102 countries took part to the negotiations. See World Trade Organization (2005: 16)

[3] Among all the other previous rounds, the Uruguay trade talks (1986-1994) were the first successful attempts in which countries agreed to substantially reform their agricultural policies.

[4] McCalla (1993: 1104)

[5] Warley (1989: 12)

per cent of world trade[6] cause so much trouble? What causes states to have so much difficulty in freeing agricultural trade? Will it ever change? If it does not, does it really matter? These questions beg a further question about how well a stalemate in agricultural trade liberalization can affect the liberalization of other areas such as services and intellectual property rights and the potential costs and benefits pertaining thereto.

Scholars who research in the field of agricultural trade share the view that this sector is a mess. Johnson has said so three times, first in 1950, when he documented the inconsistencies of trade and domestic agricultural policies. Two editions of *World Agricultural in Disarray*, published in 1973 and 1991, tell a story of resource misallocation, high consumer and fiscal costs, and distorted domestic and world markets. Johnson laments in the second edition that, if anything, the situation he described in 1973 has gotten worse. Tyers and Anderson also used the term 'disarray' in the title of their book, *Disarray in World Food Markets* (1992). Paarlberg, in his book *Fixing Farm Trade* (1988), titles his first chapter 'Agricultural Trade in Disarray'. McCalla's article "Agricultural Trade Liberalization: The Ever-Elusive Grail" (1993) qualifies negotiations on agricultural trade liberalization as a grail, which he defines as "an object of an extended or difficult quest."[7]

These are but a small sampling of books and articles produced over the past decades that have documented the major trade distortions caused by domestic agricultural support programs. Other recent monographs include the Organization for Economic Cooperation and Development (OECD), the World Bank, the International Monetary Fund (IMF), or the World Trade Organization (WTO) publications. Adding to these are literally hundreds of articles, papers, and speeches which address the same problem. Why then yet another research on the same subject? In my view there are at least three good reasons for that: First, many writers focus on the Uruguay

---

[6] Schott (1994: 43)

[7] McCalla (1993: 1102)

Round, or at most on the last three rounds of GATT negotiations (Kennedy, Tokyo and the Uruguay Rounds) whereas, this study solely deals with negotiations during the Doha Round. Second, publications of the World Bank, IMF or OECD focus much more on the positive effect of agricultural trade liberalization on poverty reduction. In doing so, they fail to investigate the roots of the deadlock.[8] Third, this study does not attempt to include other areas such as services or intellectual property rights in the inquiry; it solely focuses on agricultural trade liberalization, whose three pillars are summarized below.

## 1.1. The Three Pillars of Agricultural Trade Liberalization

Negotiations on agriculture during the Uruguay Round were conducted alongside three main areas. These are the market access, domestic support, and export subsidies commitments.[9]

### *1.1.1. Market Access*

Concerning the first pillar of *market access*, tariffication [the conversion of non-tariff barriers to equivalent bound tariffs] was one of the most important outcomes. Before the Uruguay Round, some agricultural imports were restricted by quotas and other non-tariff measures. This system was replaced by tariffs that provide more-or-less equivalent levels of protection.[10] The adoption of a tariff-only approach for agriculture was a sweeping reform that went a long way toward subjecting agricultural trade to the same disciplines applied to other traded goods such as manufactured products. Once non-tariff measures were converted into bound tariffs, developed countries

---

[8] Such estimations can be found in *The Financial Express* (2005a; 2007a)

[9] Read the respective Articles IV, VI, and VIII of the Agriculture Agreement (LT/UR/A-A1/2).

[10] For instance, if the previous policy meant domestic prices were 75 per cent higher than world prices, then the new tariff could be around 75 per cent. See WTO (2005: 27)

committed themselves to decrease average tariffs on agricultural products by a minimum of 36 per cent, in equal steps over six years (1995-2000) from their 1986-88 levels. Countries had the flexibility in structuring the 'cuts' for individual products: tariffs could be cut by much more than the average for some products and by much less for others, as long as the minimum cut per product was not below 15 per cent over the six years implementation period. For developing countries, the reductions must average 24 per cent over ten years (1995-2004) with a minimum cut of 10 per cent per product.[11] Least developed Countries did not have to cut their tariffs.

However, for products whose non-tariff restrictions had been converted to tariffs, governments were allowed to take special emergency actions in order to prevent swiftly falling prices or surges in imports from hurting their farmers.[12] Countries were allowed to impose either volume or price safeguard measures, but both could not be imposed concurrently.[13] In addition to the 'special safeguard' commitments, some countries required a 'special treatment' for their most protected products during the implementation period. Nevertheless, they agreed to establish 'minimum access' import quotas, equal to 3 per cent of domestic consumption and rising to 5 per cent at the end of the sixth year (for developed countries) and of the tenth year (for developing countries) in areas where imports had faced prohibitive trade barriers in the past.[14] As a result of the minimum access commitments, countries had to import modest amounts of their most protected products. Consequently, this commitment exposes domestic consumers to new sources of supply, increases demand for such products, and supports fur-

---

11 Schott (1994: 50); WTO (2005: 27)

12 These ,Special Safeguard Provisions' are codified in Article V of the AoA.

13 If the volume of imports rose above a certain trigger level, the importing country could impose temporary duties of up to one-third the normal applicable tariff for the duration of the marketing year; and if the price of imports fell below a trigger price equal to the average 1986 to 1988 reference price, the importing country could impose an additional duty. For more details, see Schott (1994: 51)

14 Some of these countries are Japan, Republic of Korea and the Philippines for rice; and Israel for sheep meat, whole milk powder and certain cheeses. See WTO (2005: 28); and Schott (1994: 51)

ther liberalization. The tariffication process contained also a system of 'tariff-rate-quota' (TRQ) for the specified products, with the *in-quota rate*, that is, lower tariff rates for specified quantities and *out-of-quota rate*, that is, higher rates for quantities that exceed the agreed upon quota.

### *1.1.2. Domestic Support*

The second pillar of *domestic support* was also recognised as one source of market distortions. The main complaint about policies which support domestic prices, or subsidize production in some other way, is that they encourage over-production that squeezes out imports or leads to export subsidies and low-price dumping on world markets. The Agreement on Agriculture distinguishes between support programmes that stimulate production directly, and those that are considered to have no direct effect. Developed and developing countries, therefore, agreed to limit domestic policies presumed to be the most trade distorting and to exempt other policies from any limitations. WTO members calculated how much support their governments provide to producers per year for the agricultural sector (calculated as the 'Aggregate Measure of Support', or 'Total AMS'[15]). Developed countries agreed to limit support for trade distorting domestic policies by 20 per cent of the 1986-88 support levels over six years, starting from 1995. Developing countries agreed to make 10 per cent cuts over ten years (1995-2004).[16] Least Developed Countries did not need to make any cuts.

In WTO terminology, subsidies in general are identified by 'boxes' which are given the colours of traffic lights: green (permitted), amber (slow down, or be reduced), red (forbidden). However, the Agriculture Agreement has no red box, although domestic support exceeding the reduction commitment levels in the amber box is prohibited. Instead, there is a blue box for subsi-

---

[15] The Total AMS is calculated by combining direct payments and price support benefits that directly influence production decisions. However, programs such as the US deficiency payments and EC compensation payments are exempted from the AMS calculation. See Schott (1994: 49)

dies that are tied to programmes that limit production. Hence, the AMS commitments falls under the category 'amber box', which means that trade distorting domestic support have to be slowed down. Other measures with minimal impact on trade can be used freely. They are given in the 'green box' and include government services such as research, disease control, infrastructure, food security and aid; assistance to help farmers restructure agriculture, and direct payments under environmental and regional assistance programmes that do not stimulate production.[17] Other direct payments to farmers that aim at limiting production are also permitted. Such payments fall under the 'blue box' measures and include government assistance programmes to encourage agricultural and rural development in developing countries, and other support on a small scale called *de minimis*. Developed countries were allowed to use product specific *de minimis* support if it did not exceed 5 per cent of the value of the production of that commodity, and non-product specific support where it did not exceed 5 per cent of the value of the country's total agricultural production. For developing countries, the *de minimis* level was 10 per cent, and specified agricultural input subsidies were excluded from the AMS.[18]

### *1.1.3. Export Subsidies*

Regarding the third pillar of *export subsidies*, the Agriculture Agreement imposed meaningful disciplines on agricultural export subsidies. Under the AoA, countries that employ export subsidies for agricultural commodities agreed to lower the volume and the value of their subsidies. Taking averages for 1986-90 as the base-level, developed countries agreed to cut the value of export subsidies by 36 per cent and to reduce the quantities of subsidized exports by 21 per cent over the six years (1995-2000). For Developing countries the percentage cuts were 24 and 14 per cent, respectively, in equal instalments over 10 years (1995-2004). Just like with domes-

---

16 WTO (2005: 28f); Schott (1994: 49)

17 WTO (2005: 29)

18 Read Articles VI of the AoA; and Schott (1994: 49)

tic support, Least Developed Countries did not need to make any cuts. WTO members agreed that during the implementation period, new subsidies should not be introduced. Genuine food aids for some poorest countries and export market promotion, as well as, advisory services were exempted. However, the use of marketing practices to circumvent export subsidy commitments was restricted.[19]

After the Agriculture Agreement was enforced, countries committed themselves to a continuing process of policy reform and agreed to re-launch trade negotiations by the year 2000 to build on the reforms implemented to that date.[20] As agricultural trade liberalization was considered to be an 'on-going process', member states agreed to engage in long-term objective of substantial progressive reductions in support and protection of agricultural trade. The year 2000 was considered a good opportunity for assessing the reforms so far implemented. But, how far was this reform package enforced?

## 1.2. Relevance of the Research Question

Negotiations on agricultural trade liberalization were re-launched in early 2000 under Article XX of the Agreement on Agriculture. These negotiations continued during the fourth session of the WTO Ministerial Conference held in Doha (Qatar), from 9 to 14 September 2001.[21] Divergent opinions emerged among delegates of the different countries during this Ministerial Conference. The contending issue was to know whether it was appropriate to include 'new issues' into the Doha Agenda as long as 'old issues' such as services and agriculture were still pending. During the first WTO Ministerial Conference in Singapore (1996), the EC pushed to extend the scope of negotiations by introducing new issues in investment, competition, govern-

---

19 USDA 2003a (http://www.ers.usda.gov/briefing/wto/exptsubs.htm, on 26.02.2007)

20 Read Article XX of the AoA.

21 WT/MIN(01)/DEC/1, Para. 13-14.

ment procurement, and trade facilitation into the WTO agenda.[22] These four issues are referred to as the 'Singapore issues' or 'new issues'. They are essentially about removing any domestic legislation in developing countries that favours local companies over foreign ones. Developing countries pledged for the completion of negotiations on old issues before any new issues could be introduced into the agenda. During the Doha Ministerial Conference, developing countries expressed their concern about the low speed in which any commitments made during the Uruguay Round was evolving and made it clear that introducing new issues into the agenda would simply overload it. A delegate from the developing country criticized the projections put forward by supporters of the Uruguay Round in this way: "the advantages we were supposed to gain from the Uruguay Round have not materialized."[23] Additionally, developing countries generally emphasized the need for greater market access for agricultural products in the developed world, as well as, the need to make Special and Differential Treatment (SDT) for developing countries more meaningful.[24] A Cairns Group member described how the issue of agriculture was eventually solved in the afternoon of 13 November 2001: "The EC made it clear that if they did not obtain a 'get-out' clause in agriculture they were going to walk out and there would be no deal, so we had to accept the clause, although there was some very tough exchanges of words at this stage."[25] After such intense discussion and contradictory views on how to liberalize agricultural trade, the various delegations accepted the document of the Doha Ministerial Conference with more or less enthusiasm. The EC said the document was a good compromise, South Africa urged everyone to support the Doha Agenda, Kenya pro-

---

[22] The US and the EC had different views concerning these new issues. Of the four issues, the USA supported only 'transparency in government procurement' and 'trade facilitation'. See Jawara and Kwa (2004: 39, 101)

[23] Cited by WTO (2002), the name of the delegate was withheld.

[24] Jawara and Kwa (2004: 55-69)

[25] Cited by Ibid. (p. 103), the name of the Cairns Group member was withheld.

claimed Doha a success, and several Latin American countries accepted the text.[26]

However, just some months after the Doha Ministerial was concluded, on 13 May 2002, the US Senate passed a Farm Subsidy Bill which promised to US farmers US$190 billion over the following ten years (2002-2012), an enormous increase of about 70 per cent in payments, making loans and direct payments available immediately.[27] The bill focused mainly on cotton, wheat, corn, soya, rice, barley, oats and sorghum. These payments to farmers were to rise, if world commodity prices continued to fall; they intended to provide a safety net for US farmers and to depress world prices by furthermore.[28] This bill made it clear that the USA, far from reducing agricultural subsidies, intended to use the money at its disposal to increase its markets abroad. While introducing the bill, President Bush explained this measure as follows: "Let me put it as plainly as I can: we want to be selling our beef and our corn and our beans to people around the world who need to eat."[29] This bill provoked a wave of international criticism from different parties engaged in the Doha negotiations. The heads of the three main international economic institutions, Mike Moore (WTO), James Wolfensohn (World Bank), and Horst Koehler (IMF) released a statement on 16 May 2002 that condemned the possible rise of protectionism. As predicted, in October 2002, Germany and France indeed proved that this fear was legitimate. The French President and the German Chancellor made it clear that EC dumping would continue until at least 2013 and agreed that there will be no decrease in EC agricultural subsidies, and that direct farm aid would be phased in from 2004 for the ten countries to accede to the EC by that year. From 2007 to 2013, spending will be frozen at the 2006 levels.[30] To justify the EC farm subsidies, the EC Trade Commissioner Pascal

---

26 Read Ibid. (p. 108)
27 Oxfam (2002a: 12)
28 Jawara and Kwa (2004: 139)
29 Ibid. (p. 139)
30 Mathiason (2003)

Lamy[31] said on a visit to Africa that "what the European Union did with its money was its business."[32] This change in the USA and EC agricultural policy after the Doha Ministerial Conference contradicted with their intention to advance in negotiations on the liberalization of agricultural trade. Instead of cutting their agricultural subsidies as expected, the USA and the EC did the opposite, what lead some critical observers to consider agricultural trade a unique sector in which 'liberalization' has meant an increase in subsidization.[33] Due to this policy, member states of the G20 continue to loose global markets and face ruinous competition from subsidized exports in local markets. Latin American countries said that the massive increase in US agricultural subsidies would hurt export sectors vital to their economies and vowed to fight it vigorously with tooth and nail at the WTO.

At the Cancún Ministerial Conference of 2003, no breakthrough was possible and negotiations were halted without any formal declaration.[34] To date, member states of the WTO continue to use export subsidies, and other kinds of domestic supports at levels higher than those prescribed by the Agriculture Agreement. Prior to 2005, the US Trade Representative (USTR) warned that if the EC did not cut down its export subsidies, the Congress might vote against the further participation of the US to the multilateral trading system of the WTO.[35] In recent past, bilateral trade agreements have emerged that compete with the multilateral trading system. On July 2006, Doha talks over global trade subsidies and barriers were halted after "major powers locked horns over politically sensitive issues, especially calls to dis-

---

31 Pascal Lamy became General-Director of the WTO in 2005.

32 Kahn (2002)

33 Read Oxfam (2002d: 112); Mathiason (2003)

34 Sharma (2005)

35 In the US legislation, Congress does not negotiate trade deals, but it ratifies or rejects agreement. The trade promotion authority of the US President, also known as 'fast track', allows the White House to negotiate trade deals that Congress must approve or reject without making changes. The fast track was to be renewed on June 30, 2007. See Reuters 2007b.

mantle agricultural protection."[36] It is reported from different sources that the cost of failure of an unsuccessful Doha Round will lead to increased protectionism, bilateralism and 'dirty' politics through divide-and-rule policies of the powerful states.[37] Within the WTO itself, different countries continue to build coalitions, as they strive to give their stances more weight in the bargains. Why it is so difficult to make a deal in agricultural trade liberalization? In order to answer this question, this research will analyse the negotiation strategy of the USA, the EC, and the G20 respectively.

## 1.3. Research Design

The research question of this study is 'why is agricultural trade liberalization at a stalemate?' This question entails two variables: 'stalemate' is the dependent variable and 'agricultural trade liberalization', the independent variable. In other words, the attempt to liberalize agricultural trade leads to the stalemate. However, the units of analysis here are countries themselves and not the outcome of their interaction – liberalization. The question can therefore clearly be stated as follows: why do negotiations between states – whose aim is to liberalize agricultural trade – lead to a stalemate? In order to answer that question, the United States, the European Community and the G20 were chosen as the units of analysis. The rationale behind this choice follows three general criteria of research design: plenitude (evidence), boundedness (non-arbitrariness, coherence), representativeness (external validity, as opposed to selection bias).[38]

*Plenitude* is a criterion that answers the question of how many cases does the researcher need for answering the question at hand, how large is the sample? The three groups of countries chosen here represent a large sam-

36 Reuters (2007a)
37 Mehta (2005)
38 Gerring (2001: 164)

ple of the WTO member states.[39] The EC includes 27 member states; the USA stands alone as a single state; and the G20 is represented by twenty states and more.[40] The choice of these countries allows a comparative reference point that constitutes evidence.

*Boundedness* is another general criterion that answers the question whether the specified sampling includes relevant cases and excludes irrelevant ones? There exist different coalitions within the WTO. However, the most assertive ones include the Cairns Group of states[41], the G77[42], the G20[43], and the G90[44]. The choice of the USA, the EC and the G20 as units

---

39 The membership of the WTO expands over time. At the time of writing, 151 states were members of the multilateral trading system.

40 Other developing countries joined the G20 after the Cancún Ministerial, what has expanded the group to more than twenty countries. Sometimes the group is also referred to as the G21, G22, G23 or simply G20+. See Jawara and Kwa (2004: XXVIII, footnote 1)

41 The Cairns Group is a coalition of 14 developed and developing countries, led by Australia. The group was created in 1986 during the Uruguay Round with the primary objective to eliminate export subsidies in agricultural products. Member states are Canada, New Zealand, Australia, Hungary, Brazil, Argentina, Colombia, Chile, Thailand, Fiji, Indonesia, Malaysia, Philippines, and Uruguay. See Paarlberg (1997: 432)

42 The Group of Seventy-Seven was established by seventy-seven developing countries in June 1964 at the end of the first meeting of the United Nations Conference on Trade and Development (UNCTAD) in Geneva. The G77 defines its objective as threefold: to articulate and promote the collective economic interests of its members; to enhance its joint negotiating capacity on major economic issues, and to promote economic and technical cooperation among developing countries. The group has expanded to more than 113 countries, but it is still referred to as the G77, see www.g77.org.

43 The G20/G20+ is a powerful new bloc of developing countries which came on its own at the Cancún trade talks in September 2003. It is united by clearly articulated economic interests on whom it negotiates forcefully with the USA and the EC. The alliance includes most of the world's most populous countries and most of its fastest growing economies. Member states are Argentina, Bolivia, Brazil, Chile, China, Cuba, Egypt, Guatemala, India, Indonesia, Mexico, Nigeria, Pakistan, Paraguay, Philippines, South Africa, Thailand, Tanzania, Uruguay, Venezuela, and Zimbabwe. See Wade, in Ravenhill (2005: 320); Jawara and Kwa (2004: XV)

of analysis can be justified by three main reasons. First, with 25 per cent of agricultural exports, the USA is the main exporter of agricultural products on the world,[45] while the EC is the main importer and the second exporter of agricultural products on world markets;[46] the G20 is composed of the most populous countries in the world such as India, China, Brazil, Indonesia, Nigeria, Malaysia, and South Africa. This last group of countries, although not having a big share of agricultural trade on world markets, could become strong challengers of the USA and the EC if the sector was liberalized. Second, the G77 and G90 were excluded because they do not have a strong bargaining power in the negotiations. Many of their member states are exempted from the commitments in the tariff cuts negotiations (all the LDCs), while others demand Special and Differential Treatment. As reciprocity is an integral part of the bargaining in international trade relations, countries that are not able to give something in return, after having received from others, have limited influence on the negotiation process.[47] The third reason why the Cairns Group of states was not included in the analysis is that, although it played an important role during the Uruguay Round (1986-1994), the group does not necessarily do so during the period under investigation here (2001-2006). The Cairns Group – previously the third force in agricultural negotiations during the Uruguay Round – had been undermined by deep splits between those who wanted major tariff reductions (mainly OECD countries), and others who prioritized defending their domestic markets against imports (mainly developing countries).[48] In addition, member states of the OECD, Canada, New Zealand, Australia, and Hungary may not face the same difficulties to access other OECD domestic markets as developing countries of this group do. This situation may explain why all developing countries but Fiji left the group in 2003 and created the G20. For

---

44 The G90 is a coalition of Least Developed Countries (LDCs), the African, Caribbean, and Pacific (ACP) group, and the African Union (AU). The group re-emerged during the Cancún Ministerial in 2003. See Jawara and Kwa (2004: XV)

45 Oxfam (2002a: 12)

46 European Communities (2004: 24)

47 Read Article XXVIII bis of GATT; and Keohane (1986)

48 Jawara and Kwa (2004: XXVII)

these above-mentioned reasons, the USA, the EC and the G20 were chosen as relevant cases that can better explain the stalemate in agricultural trade liberalization.

The last criterion for this research design is *representativeness*, which refers to the comparability between the sample and the population. There are two ways of achieving representativeness: "first, one may choose cases randomly from the population of potential cases. Properly conducted, randomization procedures maximize the representativeness of a given sample [...] second, one might choose *all* possible cases, in which circumstances there is no problem of representativeness."[49] As cases were chosen randomly from the population, there is a problem of representativeness posed in this study. Is the sample representative of the population of the WTO? In order to answer this question, countries from the developed as well as the developing world were taken into account: the USA and the EC represent the developed, while the G20 represents the developing world. The sample includes different regions of the world, as well. From the developed world, Europe is represented by the EC, North America by the USA. And from the developing world, Latin America is represented by Argentina, Bolivia, Chile, Brazil, Paraguay, Uruguay, Venezuela; Asia is represented by India, China, Indonesia, Pakistan, Philippines, Thailand; Central American and the Caribbean countries by Mexico, Guatemala, Cuba; and finally Africa by Egypt, Nigeria, South Africa and Zimbabwe. Nevertheless, representativeness could have been achieved by using another sampling strategy.[50]

---

49 Gerring (2001: 181)

50 It was also possible to sample, for example, one country from each economic region of the world, using an extreme-case, crucial-case, or typical-case study. Or simply choose all the possible cases, and therefore overrule the problem of representativeness, since N would be equalled to the whole population, see Gerring (2001: Chap. 9)

## 1.4. Organization of the Study

This study is divided into seven chapters. The first chapter, which is composed of four sections, is a general introduction. Section (1.1) deals with the three pillars of agricultural trade liberalization, market access, domestic support, and export subsidies. Section (1.2) focuses on the relevance of the research question; section (1.3) works out three general criteria of research design, *plenitude*, *boundedness*, and *representativeness*, to explain the choice of the sample. Finally, section (1.4) is the organisational part. Chapter two discusses two theories: the liberal theory of International Relations at the one hand; and the classical, neo-classical and modern trade theories at the other. The liberal theory of IR asks the question whether preferences matter, whereas, classical, neoclassical and modern trade theories tackle the issue of income distribution effects of trade and work out the concept of strategic trade policies. The third chapter analyses the dynamic of negotiations between the three groups of countries. Section (3.1) answers the question 'what is multilateralism' while section (3.2), which is in turn subdivided into three subsections, deals with the logic of two-level games. Subsections (3.2.1), (3.2.2), and (3.2.3) respectively deal with the dynamic of negotiations in the USA, in the EC, and in the G20. For each group of countries, its respective agricultural policy will be introduced prior to 2001, before presenting the negotiations during the period under inquiry. Chapter four is about the outcome of negotiations. Here, section (4.1) deals with the July Package and section (4.2) which is also subdivided into two subsections, deals with implementation-related concerns. Subsection (4.2.1) depicts the stalemate in agricultural trade liberalization as a collective action problem, while subsection (4.2.2) conceives it as a prisoner's dilemma. Chapter five is concerned with the agricultural policy reform of the USA, the EC, and their impact on member states of the G20. Based on empirical case studies, sections (5.1) and (5.2) ask the question how effectively the USA and the EC implemented the agricultural reforms of the Uruguay Round, while section (5.3) works out the impact of such reforms or the lack thereof on the G20 farming sector. Chapter six is an attempt to find a way out of the stalemate. Here section (6.1) takes over the question about the size of the win-sets and subsection (6.1.1) deals with internal side-payments and synergic linkages, as part of the solution. In the last chapter, the study will be concluded and its main findings pointed out.

## 2. Do Preferences Matter?

International negotiations generally follow two steps: one step involves the formation of preferences of actors and the other, interaction among actors that leads to an outcome.[51] This study highlights the interaction among actors and avoid explaining actor's preference formation; it assumes that preferences are exogenously given and that in situations of decision-making, each actor will intentionally choose the one alternative that promises the best realization of the own interests.[52]

According to the liberal theory of international relations (IR), the configuration of state preferences is what matters most in world politics. The liberal theory "rests on a 'bottom up' view of politics in which the demands of individuals and societal groups are treated as analytically prior to politics."[53] Scholars of the IR theory distinguish between a 'bottom-up' and a 'top-down' approach of international politics. The bottom-up view of international relations, to which the liberal theory of IR subscribes, bases its core assumption on the view that individuals make politics. In order to understand what happens at the global level, it is necessary to analyse individuals' behaviours at the domestic realm. Whereas the top-down approach (realists and neo-realists) bases its assumption on the reasoning that states are the main focus of analysis in world politics, the liberal theory assumes that states are just 'transmission belts' by which the preferences and social power of individuals and groups are translated into state policy. For liberals, states are constantly *captured* and *recaptured* by the different coalitions of social actors. Government policy is "constrained by the underlying identi-

---

51 Legro (1996: 118). Actors can be individual actors as well as states.

52 According to rational choice theory, each actor aims at maximizing its strategic utility in situations of decision-making processes. Utility refers to an actor's subjective assessment of the benefits of a particular outcome or course of action. See Aggarwal and Dupont, in Ravenhill (2005: 32)

53 Moravcsik (1997: 517)

ties, interests, and power of individuals and groups (inside and outside the state apparatus) who constantly pressure the central decision makers to pursue policies consistent with their preferences."[54] This is not to adopt a pluralist view of domestic politics in which all identities and interests are represented at the national level, or one in which all individuals and groups have equal influence on the state. Every government can only represent some individuals and groups at the expense of some others. Therefore, it does not matter, whether only the interests of a dictator (autocracy) are represented in negotiations, or those of a particular societal group (democracy). Based on those grounds, the liberal theory is capable of explaining negotiations in situations where both authoritarian and democratic negotiators are involved. Furthermore, the liberal theory does not ignore the role state institutions play in shaping domestic demands, then "between theoretical extremes of tyranny and democracy, many representative institutions and practices exist, each of which privileges particular demands; hence the nature of state institutions, alongside societal interests themselves, is a key determinant of what states do internationally."[55] Politics at the domestic level is central to understanding world politics, from a liberal point of view. But what drives the emergence of domestic interest groups in the first place? This question will be answered in light of the theory of income distributional effect of trade.

## 2.1. Lobbying Incentives: Income Distribution Effects of Trade

Classical trade theories of Adam Smith and David Ricardo assume that international trade increases national welfare. In *An Inquiry into the Nature and Causes of the Wealth of Nations* (1776), Adam Smith wrote: "If a foreign country can supply us with a commodity cheaper that we ourselves can make it, better buy it of them with some part of the produce of our own

---

54 Ibid. (p. 518)
55 Ibid. (p. 518)

industry, employed in a way in which we have some advantage."[56] The rationale behind such exchange of goods can be explained as follows: if a foreign country B can produce some goods at lower costs than a home country A, and if country A can also produce some other sets of goods at lower costs than country B, then it will be best for country B to trade its cheaper goods for country A relatively cheaper goods. In this way, both countries can gain from trade: this is the theory of trade according to *absolute advantage*. Moreover, this theory raised some controversies among nations that feared international trade may leave them worst off, because they do not have absolute advantage in any sector of the economy. It was until the publication of David Ricardo's book *The Principles of Political Economy and Taxation* (1817) that this fear was mitigated. Ricardo ascertained that absolute advantage was a limited case of more general basis for international trade and introduced the concept of *comparative advantage,* instead. The logic of comparative advantage rests on the *opportunity costs* of producing goods across countries, that is, the amount of one good that has to be given up to produce another good. Ricardo demonstrated that it was in the interests of two countries to trade, even if one country had an absolute advantage so that it could produce all goods more cheaply than the other. He showed that by concentrating on areas where they had a comparative advantage – the area in which they were most efficient – two countries could arrive at a higher level of wealth by exchanging two goods than if they each produced both goods.

The theory of comparative advantage was further expanded in a two-country, two-factor of production model by Heckscher and Ohlin.[57] The two-country, two-factor model assumes that "a country will export those com-

---

56 Smith 1976 (Book IV, Section ii: 12)

57 Eli Heckscher and Bertil Ohlin were two Swedish economists. Heckscher was the professor and Ohlin his student. The Heckscher-Ohlin model is a general equilibrium model of international trade that assumes two or more countries and clearly shows that, in the case of free trade, each country exports the good for which it en-

modities which are produced with its relatively abundant factors of production, and will import those in the production of which its relatively scarce factors are important."[58] For illustration, if the USA and India were to trade for instance, the theory states that, although, the USA may have an absolute advantage in producing both capital-intensive goods such as computers, and labour-intensive goods such as textiles and apparel, given her opportunity costs in the production of capital-intensive goods, it would be better for the USA to specialize in the production of those goods and India in the production of labour-intensive goods. If the USA exchanges her cheap computers against Indian cheap textiles and apparel, both countries could be better off, all other things being equal. The theory concludes, therefore, that free trade would make it possible for both households to consume more goods, regardless of whether their trade partner was more or less advanced.

Applied in today's economy, however, the theory of comparative advantage generates great controversy. Ricardo provided a *specific factors model,* in which factors of production are specific to a particular industry and when that industry declines as the result of trade, its factors can not move to the rising industry. But factors of production such as skills and resources are not specific to any industry. If they were fixed, countries like the USA would never have moved beyond her comparative advantage in land availability and would have remained an agricultural economy. Another problem linked to the theory of comparative advantage is that international market conditions have changed, since Ricardo assumed that capital did not move between countries, that trade would take place between competing companies, and that markets were not exposed to imperfect competition. In today's economy however, capital is global; a growing share of trade takes place within firms, within the same industry, and within regional blocs. Additionally, concentrations of market power at national and international levels

---

joys a comparative advantage. See Van den Berg (2004: 88); Stolper and Samuelson (1941)

create restrictive barriers. This theory falls short to answer the question why some individuals or groups, within the same country, oppose trade liberalization and others do not.

In 1941, Wolfgang Stolper and Paul Samuelson derived a theorem that explains trade policy preferences within countries. The Stolper-Samuelson theorem states that when an economy opens its borders to free trade,

> the introduction of trade will increase the production of those commodities which use relatively much of the abundant factor, and will lower the production of the commodities using relatively little of the abundant factor. Accompanying this, there will be the familiar Heckscher-Ohlin tendency towards partial equalization of factor prices in the two countries, the price of the scarce falling in relationship to the price of the abundant factor.[59]

With free trade, the production of the scarce factor will shrink while the production of the abundant factor will increase. As a consequence, the real incomes of the owners of the factor that is used less intensively will fall and the real incomes of the owners of the intensively used factors will increase, what leads to income distributional effects of trade.[60]

In the specific factors model, distributional consequences of international trade affect industries rather than factors. Both the labour and capital employed in some industries gain from trade, while the labour and capital employed in other industries both loose from trade. Thus, *import-competing industries* will lobby for protectionist measures and the *export-competing industries* for trade liberalization. Moreover, when factors of production are mobile between sectors, owners of the same factor have the same chance

---

58 Read Stolper and Samuelson (1941: 58f)

59 Stolper and Samuelson (1941: 70) For more details on how factor prices are equalized, read Samuelson (1948); Oatley (2004: 89)

60 The theorem states that not only does the price of the abundant factor rise with free trade, but the real value of the income earned by the abundant factor also rises. Whether this prediction holds when tested to empirical cases is another issue.

to its return, regardless of whether it is employed in the protected industry or not. Therefore, the conflict is between the factors of production, regardless of the industry in which they work. In countries where the abundant factor is 'capital' and the scarce factor 'labour', the owners of capital will be the winners of free trade while the owners of the scarce factor labour will be the losers. As a consequence, the owners of labour will pressure their government to adopt protectionist measures and the owners of capital will pressure for liberalizing policies.

With classical models of trade theory, economies were assumed to be characterised by constant returns to scale and perfect competition. The traditional Ricardian model emphasizes differences in technology and tastes as causes of trade, the Heckscher-Ohlin model stresses the conflicts of interest between both the owners of the abundant factors and of the scarce factors of production, while the Stolper-Samuelson models emphasizes factor price change as the consequence of trade. Income distribution effects are absent in the Ricardian model, but extremely strong in the Heckscher-Ohlin-Samuelson model.

Since the late 1970s, modern trade theories have emerged that explain the possibility of trade for reasons other than exogenous differences in tastes, technology, and factor endowments. These models establish the idea that countries specialize and trade, not only because of underlying differences, but also because increasing returns to scale are independent forces that lead to geographical concentration of production of each good. The new view introduced was the *strategic trade policy* argument, and the idea that government should favour *external economies* of scale.[61]

According to Krugman, the strategic trade policy argument begins with the observation that a country can raise its national income, if it can somehow

---

[61] Krugman (1987: 134)

ensure that the lucky firm[62] that gets to earn excess returns is a domestic rather than a foreign firm. Therefore, under certain circumstances a government, by supporting its firm in international competition, can raise national welfare at another country's expense. Proponents of the new trade theory like Michael Spence, Avinash Dixit, or Joseph Stiglitz are of the view that this goal can be achieved via a financial support or export subsidy and other policies as well.[63] For example, when there is a significant domestic market for a good, protection of this market raises the profit of the domestic firm at the expense of the foreign firm in the case where both enter the market. Therefore, if the government targets some sectors of the economy in providing them with subsidies, it may be able to earn returns higher than the opportunity costs of the resources they employ as well as deter new entries. Instead of sharing the domestic market with foreign competing firms, it is better to protect that market from new entries; what allows domestic firms to capture the excess returns at the expense of foreign entrants.[64]

Another argument of the new trade theory is that government policy should favour industries that yield externalities, especially generation of knowledge. Investment in knowledge has fixed-cost aspects. Once a firm has improved its technique of production, the unit cost of that improvement falls as more is produced. The result of these dynamic economies of scale leads to the breakdown of perfect competition because inefficient and marginal producers are driven out of the market. Moreover, as knowledge may spill over between countries, foreign firms can "reverse engineer" a foreign technology. In this case, there will be a tendency for some countries to protect that knowledge.[65]

---

62 Read ‚first stage processing firm' here. First stage processors specialized in the production of agricultural goods such as sugar or cotton also yield increasing returns to scale, as it will be made clear in chapter 5.

63 Krugman (1987: 133-136)

64 Ibid. (p. 136)

To sum up, while traditional trade theories hold that trade is driven by comparative advantage, constant returns to scale and perfect competition, new trade theories assume that trade is to an important degree driven by increasing returns to scale and that international markets are typically imperfectly competitive. Both theories, however, share the view that trade is of mutual benefit to the trading nations. As far as trade theory is concerned, one can therefore agree with Krugman that "free trade is not passé – but it is not what it once was."[66]

Another recent trade theory that analyses the income distributional effect of trade in the agricultural sector is the study by Anderson and Hayami (1986). In this study, the authors adopt a cosmopolitan approach to explain why all industrial societies tend to protect farmers and conclude that, largely apart from a country's unique history, culture, or institutions, the level of agricultural protection tends to rise with industrialization, or more precisely "as comparative advantage shifts away from agriculture."[67] As comparative advantage shifts away from agriculture to industry, the focus of public policy protection will shift from industry to agriculture. This approach not only predicts that farmers will receive protection; it also predicts the average level of that protection, for instance which crops will be protected the most. Therefore, comparatively advantaged *export-competing crops* will be less protected than comparatively disadvantaged *import-competing crops.* If this theory holds, it may imply two things. On the one hand, one may expect the US and EC farmers to lobby for protectionist measures. On the other hand, one may also expect some groups of farmers to protect specific crops

---

65 The protection of knowledge can lead to the protection of a whole firm from intruders who are likely to 'steal' the knowledge, what may stir up the incentives to protect the industry or even the domestic market as a whole.

66 Krugman (1987: 143)

67 Anderson and Hayami (1986: 45)

within the farm industry. Additionally, one will expect the G20's manufacturers to oppose free trade.[68]

The next chapter deals with the dynamic of agricultural trade negotiations between the three groups of countries under inquiry here. Will the above-mentioned theories help better explain the lobbying incentives of the different individuals and groups within the respective countries?

68 The trade theories referred to in this section are nothing but a small sample of theories that researchers have developed over the last centuries. I only mentioned those of interest for my study, acknowledging that I could include more.

# 3. Dynamic of Negotiations

This chapter starts with a brief definition of multilateralism. Thereafter, it follows a theory of international negotiations, upon which the dynamic of trade negotiations between the countries is built. Starting with the USA, the study will show that negotiations to reform her agricultural policy require a rather complicated two-level game. With the EC, the game is still more complicated as it is expanded to three levels that require high negotiating skills at the domestic, community and international levels for any change of its common agricultural policy. The G20 is a heterogeneous group of countries which has to play a two-level game in global trade negotiations, like the USA. Negotiations between these groups of countries involve the interaction among many states. When three or more states are involved in the bargaining at the international level, one speaks of multilateral negotiations. However, is multilateralism just a matter of numbers?

## 3.1. What is Multilateralism?

A sound attempt to define multilateralism was first made by Robert Keohane (1990), but his definition was considered too loose and missed the qualitative element that is central to the concept 'multilateralism'.[69] According to John Gerard Ruggie, multilateralism is not only about the number of parties involved in the interaction, but also the kind of relations that are instituted among them. He defines multilateralism as:

> an institutional form which coordinates relations among three or more states on the basis of 'generalized' principles of conduct – that is, principles which specify appropriate conduct for a class of actions, without regard to the par-

[69] See Ruggie (1992: 566)

ticularistic interests of the parties or the strategic exigencies that may exist in any specific occurrence.[70]

According to this definition, multilateralism is first of all an institution, and generically institutions are persistent and connected sets of rules, which can be formal or informal codes of conduct that prescribe behavioural roles, constrain activity, and shape expectations.[71] Second, multilateralism involves the interaction among three or more states. Third, this interaction follows generalized principles of conduct, that is, the behaviours of actors are constrained by established rules that have a general effect on all parties independent of their particularistic interests. The definition of multilateralism offered here contains both the quantitative and qualitative aspects of multilateralism consistent with the purpose of this study.

The rule governing multilateral trade is embodied in Article I of the General Agreement on Tariffs and Trade (GATT, 1994). Known as the Most-Favoured-Nation principle (MFN), this article states that "any advantage, favour, privilege or immunity granted by any contracting party to any product originating in or destined for any other country shall be accorded immediately and unconditionally to the like product originating in or destined for the territories of all other contracting parties."[72] The appropriate and generalized principles of conduct meant here concern the granting of the same privileges to all the other parties once such a prerogative has been granted to one 'favoured' member of the WTO. Three qualitative elements can be sorted out of the MFN principle: First, *any advantage* granted to one member should be extended to the others. The MFN Treatment obligation concerns advantages such as customs duties, other charges on imports and exports, internal taxes, and internal regulation affecting the sale, distribution and use of products. Second, discrimination is only prohibited in relation to *the like products*, so that products which are not 'like' may be treated differ-

---

70 Ibid. (p. 571)

71 Keohane (1990: 732)

ently. And third, the advantage should be granted *immediately and unconditionally* to imports or other commercial transactions from all other WTO members. Once a WTO member has granted an advantage to imports from a country, it cannot make it condition upon payment to the other members of the WTO.

After this brief definition of multilateralism, the following section focuses on the dynamic of agricultural trade negotiations between the USA, the EC, and the G20. An introduction to the logic of two-level games will help analyse the mechanism of trade negotiations between these groups. A full historical account of the negotiations will not be given here, but rather I focus on some salient moments of such negotiations. Hence, the analysis will start with a historical contextualization of the agricultural policy of the different countries prior to 2001, and will continue with trade negotiations under the period of inquiry.

## 3.2. The Logic of Two-Level Games

The metaphor of 'two-level games' is used for domestic-international interaction between states. In the article *Diplomacy and Domestic Politics: the Logic of Two-Level Games* (1988), Robert Putnam describes how the game unfolds:

> The politics of many international negotiations can usefully be conceived as a two-level game. At the national level, domestic groups pursue their interests by pressuring the government to adopt favourable policies, and politicians seek power by constructing coalitions among these groups. At the international level, national governments seek to maximize their own ability to satisfy domestic pressures, while minimizing the adverse consequences of foreign developments.[73]

---

[72] Art. I (GATT)

Two games emerged out of this constellation: the game played at the national level and the other played at the international one. At the international level, state officials are considered 'transmission belts' of the interests of domestic groups. To use a liberal theory's jargon, states are 'captured' by domestic coalitions whose interests and preferences are represented at the international level. State officials therefore have the difficult task to broker conflicting interests at both levels. The two games are interrelated as long as countries remain interdependent, and decision-makers cannot ignore one of them in negotiations. Following the logic of the game, every political leader has to play at different boards of the table: *across the international table* sit the foreign counterpart, *at his elbows* sit diplomats and other international advisors, and *around the domestic table behind him* sit party and parliamentary figures, representatives of different interest groups, and leader's own political advisors.[74] The complexity of this game stems from the fact that a move that seems rational for one player at one board (such as conceding tariff cuts or limiting domestic support in multilateral negotiations) may seem political inappropriate for the same player at the other board (no ratification of the agreement at the domestic level). This complexity is more apparent when it comes to secure support at home while trying to make a deal at the international table. "Any key player at the international table who is dissatisfied with the outcome may upset the game board, and conversely, any leader who fails to satisfy his fellow players at the domestic table risks being evicted from his seat."[75] Putnam calls the bargaining between the negotiators at the international realm, Level I, and discussions within each group of constituents about whether to ratify the agreement, Level II.[76] In many cases, the two-level process may be iterative, as the negotiator tries out possible agreements and probe their constituents' view. Therefore the requirement that any Level I agreement must, in the end, be ratified at Level II imposes a crucial theoretical link between the two levels.

---

73 Putnam (1988: 434)

74 Ibid. The emphasis was added by Gabriel Ngwe (G.N.)

75 Ibid.

76 Ibid. (p. 436)

According to Mo (1994), the bargaining power of the domestic constituents, which in turn depends on the political power in the domestic bargaining process, determines the size of the negotiator's domestic constraints. Such domestic bargaining process is divided into a *proposal-making process*, in which a country formulates its proposal, and a *ratification process*, through which the country ratifies an agreement.[77] Given this domestic political process, each domestic participant – including the negotiator – is assumed to have three sources of political power. First a 'preference-based power', that is, the ability to wait for a better offer that meets the own preferences; second an 'agenda-setting power', that is, the authority to make a proposal or set the agenda; and third a 'veto power', that is, the authority to veto a proposal.[78] These measures of domestic political power constitutes what Mo calls 'potential or latent power' that may not automatically translate into actual power as reflected in the outcome of international negotiations. The electorate plays a crucial role in this political process. As the economic conditions of electorate changes, so do their preferences, and the international bargaining outcome reflects those changes. However, as an indirect participant to the international bargaining, the electorate can only indirectly influence such bargaining through elections. How a country formulates its national proposal therefore involves domestic political competition between competing groups. "Domestic political competition is modelled as the competition over agenda-setting power. If a domestic group obtains agenda-setting power, its proposal becomes a national proposal in the bargaining with [other countries]."[79] The key issue for domestic interest groups is therefore to influence their national government in such a way that it adopts their own preferences as national policy at the international bargaining table. To compound the issue, a nation as a whole never makes trade policy decisions. "Citizens of a country never collectively determine (in a referendum) trade policies. [...] trade policies are not determined by a summed-up figure

77 Mo (1994: 404)

78 Ibid. (p. 405)

79 Ibid. (p. 408)

called 'national interest' based on the most efficient outcome."[80] Domestic politics is what matters. Although a particular group may dominate domestic politics, another groups' coalition could at any time challenges this constellation. Thus, the game of coalition-building at Level II is a never-ending one in which the group that has the agenda-setting power today runs the risk of loosing it tomorrow.[81]

The actors at level II may represent bureaucratic agencies, interest groups, social classes, or even public opinion such as labour unions while the actors at Level I may be government representatives. The formal constraint on the ratification of an international agreement stems from the fact that an identical agreement must be ratified by both sides. Therefore, a preliminary Level I agreement cannot be amended at Level II without reopening the Level I negotiations. In other words, final ratification must be simply 'voted up or down'; any modification to the Level I agreement introduced by one party to negotiations counts as a rejection, unless such modification is approved by all other parties to the agreement.[82] Given this set of arrangements, Putnam considers the 'win-sets' at Level II constituency to be decisive on the outcome of any ratification process. He defines win-set as "the set of all possible Level I agreements that would 'win' – that is, gain the necessary majority among the constituents – when simply voted up or down."[83] Putnam introduces two different reasons why the contours of the Level II win-sets are so important for understanding Level I agreements.

First, *larger win-sets make Level I agreement more likely,* other things being equal.[84] By definition, any successful agreement is expected to fall within the Level II win-sets of each of the party to the agreement. Thus, agreement is possible only if those win-sets overlap, the larger each of them is,

---

80 Kim and Smith (1997: 441)
81 For more details on coalition analysis, read Gourevitch (1978).
82 Putnam (1988: 437)
83 Ibid. (p. 437)
84 Ibid. The original text is emphasised.

and the more likely they are to overlap. Conversely, the smaller the win-sets are, the greater the risk that negotiations will break down.[85] Lida takes over this issue and mentions three reasons that can lead to the breakdown of negotiations. First, negotiations can break down when the win-sets of the negotiating countries do not intersect, second, when domestic approval does not occur with probability one, and finally when the win-sets change during negotiations because of domestic changes such as the change of government or government coalitions.[86]

The second reason why win-set size is important is that *the relative size of the respective Level II win-sets will affect the distribution of the joint gains from the international bargain.*[87] That is, the larger the perceived win-set of a negotiator, the more he can be 'pushed around' by the other Level I negotiators. However, a small domestic win-set can be a bargaining advantage: 'I would like to accept your proposal, but I could never get it accepted at home' is the way negotiators lament about the domestic constraints under which they operate when negotiating with international partners.[88] Precisely because of such tactics, it is better for a negotiator to ensure himself a 'negotiating room' at Level II before opening the Level I negotiations. Experienced negotiators almost invariably insist that the more difficult part in international negotiations consists not in dealing with their adversary across the table, but in handling interest groups, bureaucrats, and politicians at home; that is, securing win-sets at the domestic level.[89]

---

85 Putnam distinguishes two kinds of failed ratification here, namely *voluntary* and *involuntary defections*. Voluntary defection refers to reneging by a rational egoist in the absence of enforceable contracts; involuntary defection instead reflects the behaviour of an agent who is unable to deliver on a promise because of failed ratification by domestic constituencies, (p. 438)

86 Lida (1993: 405)

87 Putnam (1988: 440). The original text is emphasised.

88 Ibid.

89 Mayer (1992: 793)

Putnam deciphers three factors that are important to understand what circumstances affect the win-set size: First, the Level II preferences and coalitions; second the Level II institutions; and third, the Level I negotiator's strategies.[90]

The first proposition about the Level II preferences and coalition states that "*the size of the win-set depends on the distribution of power, preferences, and possible coalitions among Level II constituents.*"[91] According to Putnam, any testable two-level theory of international negotiation must take into account the theory of domestic politics, i.e., a theory about the power and preferences of the major actors at Level II. When the win-set of domestic constituent is too small, the cost of 'no-agreement' is also lower, what increases the incentives to block the ratification process at the domestic level. Then, ratification pits the proposed contract, not against an array of other possible attractive alternatives, but only against 'no-agreement'. Whereas some constituents may face low costs from no-agreement, other may face high costs. The former will be more sceptical of Level I agreements than the latter. When the costs and/or benefits of a proposed agreement are relatively concentrated, it is straightforward to expect that those constituents whose interests are most affected will exert special influence on the ratification process. As a general rule, "the group with the greatest interest in a specific issue is also likely to hold the most extreme position on that issue."[92] If each individual actor was allowed to fix the level I negotiating position for 'its' issue, the resulting package would almost surely be 'non-negotiable', that is, non-ratifiable in the different capitals. Thus, the chief negotiator is faced with different tradeoffs and plagued with alternative policy choices: how much to yield on cotton exports to get a better deal on sugar, how much to yield on banana export to get a better deal on citrus fruit. This trade-off raises the problem of issue linkage which is absolutely

---

90 Putnam (1988: 442)

91 Ibid. (p. 442). The passage is emphasised in the original text.

92 Ibid. (p. 446)

important to understanding how domestic and international politics can become entangled.

Let us suppose that a majority of constituents at Level II oppose a given policy – a cut in government transfers to sugar producers, for example – but that some members of that majority would be willing to switch their vote on that issue for more job security – high guaranteed quotas to domestic producers, a policy choice that aims at preserving more jobs. If bargaining is limited to Level II, that trade-off may seem technically not feasible, but if the chief negotiator can broker an international deal that secures high domestic sugar production, for instance through a high demand of that sugar on world markets, he can overturn the initial outcome at the domestic level and win his constituents for ratification of the deal.[93] This strategy works not by *changing the preferences of any domestic constituent*, but rather by *creating a policy option* (such as the sale of the same amount of domestic sugar production on world markets after the cuts in government transfers) that was previously beyond domestic control. Putnam calls this type of issue linkage at Level I that alters the feasible outcomes at Level II as 'synergic linkage'.[94] Interdependence multiplies the opportunities to alter domestic coalitions by expanding the set of feasible alternatives and creating entanglements across national boundaries.

The second proposition brought by Putnam states that "*the size of the win-set depends on the Level II political institutions.*"[95] Domestic political institutions also play a decisive role in the ratification process. For example, if a two-thirds vote is required for ratification, the win-set will almost certainly be smaller than if only a simple majority is required. Therefore, negotiations

---

93 The domestic constituency may be willing to accept cuts in government transfers only if it is somehow certain that jobs will be protected. If jobs can be maintained through high levels of domestic production, despite the cuts in government transfers, a deal may be possible. Otherwise the agreement will be blocked at Level II.

94 Putnam (1988: 447). The emphasis was added by G.N.

95 Ibid. (p. 448). The passage is emphasised in the original text.

were both democratic and non-democratic states are involved pose different constraints on their respective negotiators. In the United States for example, thirty-four out of hundred senators can block ratification of any treaty. The US separation of powers imposes a tighter constraint on the American win-set than in many other democratic states with simple majority voting system or in non-democratic states. This domestic constraint increases the bargaining power of US negotiators, but at the same time it reduces the scope for international cooperation and raises the scope of involuntary defection of American negotiators. If the executive branch negotiates under legislative authority, as this is the case with the 'fast track authority' in the USA, then the executive branch has a firm position that is visible to other negotiating partners. On the contrary, negotiators from non-democratic states are to some extents isolated from the pressures of their domestic interest groups, what makes it possible for such negotiators to drive a better deal with other international partners.[96]

The third and last proposition states that "*the size of the win-set depends on the strategies of the Level I negotiators*".[97] Each level I negotiator has an unequivocal interest in maximizing his win-set, then the larger his win-set, the more easily he can conclude an agreement, but also the weaker his bargaining position vis-à-vis the other negotiator. In case of a smaller win-set, it is possible to attract marginal supporters through the usage of internal side-payments. The existence of side-payment opportunities may help to reopen portions of the bargaining set blocked by domestic factions. Side-payments are "payments that redistribute value among internal factions without affecting national welfare."[98] If two crops such as sugar and cotton were produced in the same country, where sugar was the export-competing crop and cotton the import-competing one, the opening of borders to free trade could benefit the factors of production used intensively to produce sugar, other things being equal. In such a situation, the factors employed in

---

96 Ibid. (p. 440)

97 Ibid. (p. 450). The passage is emphasised in the original text.

the cotton sector may oppose free trade. In order to attract their support, one possibility is to redistribute the gains from trade in such a manner that those losers are compensated. Hence, agreements made at the international level can become possible if the parties to negotiations link side-issue internally on which to compensate potential losers from greater liberalization. Such compensation mechanism can help solve the problem of income distribution effects of trade. Internal side-payments may facilitate negotiations, although arranging them is not an easy task.[99] Most important however, is the recognition that "the availability of the side-payment may facilitate efficiency."[100]

After this theoretical part, I turn now to the evolving of negotiations between the United States, the European Community and the G20.

### *3.2.1. United States*

The current agricultural trade policy of the United States was inaugurated between 1933 and 1938. "Until the mid-1930s, both agriculture and manufactures were treated essentially alike: when either suffered economic decline, the usual state response was to increase trade barriers."[101] The crisis that preceded this shift in agricultural and manufacturing trade policy was the Great Depression. The Great Depression caused the USA to question, and restructure, the government-society relations over commercial policy. The interaction of various factors, including the impulse to use the tariff, the presence of a weak, penetrated Congress, and the depressed economy, led to the passage of the Smoot-Hawley Act of 1930.[102] By the mid-1940s, a two-pronged approach to address the problems of agriculture and manufac-

---

98 Mayer (1992: 807)

99 Ibid. (p. 816)

100 Ibid. (p. 815)

101 Goldstein (1989: 32)

102 On the political economy of the Smooth-Hawley Tariff, read Eichengreen, in Frieden and Lake (2004: 37-46)

tures was enacted. The government was to help manufacturers gain access to foreign markets through a program of reciprocal tariff reductions. Agriculture could also benefit from some tariff reductions, but largely it should be protected through a system of internal price supports and land-use policies.[103] For the majority of farm products, five laws were passed that structured agricultural policy in the United States. These are the Agricultural Adjustment Act (1933), the act creating the Commodity Credit Corporation (1933), The Soil Conservation and Domestic Allotment Act (1936), the Agricultural Marketing Agreement Act (1937), and the Agricultural Adjustment Act (1938).[104]

The *Agricultural Adjustment Act* (AAA) of 1933 authorized the Secretary of Agriculture to raise market prices in seven commodities – wheat, corn, cotton, rice, tobacco, hogs, milk and milk products – by getting producers to voluntarily reduce acreage or production. In return for reducing production, farmers would be paid for the part of their production required for domestic consumption.[105] The *Commodity Credit Corporation* (CCC) was established by executive order in 1933. The CCC was authorized to buy, hold, lend upon, or deal in any agricultural commodity designated by the President. The CCC directly affects market prices of agricultural products through non-recourse loans to producers, which can be repaid by forfeiting crops to the government if the market price at harvest time is lower than the loan rate. Under these guarantees, the US government's CCC has at times acquired large quantities of various commodities, which have been stored or donated as food aid to less developed countries.[106] The *Soil Conservation and Domestic Allotment Act* of 1936 encourages producers to 'idle land'. In return, they are paid for switching from production of surplus crops to production of

---

103 Goldstein (1989: 32)

104 Ibid. (p. 45). These are important legislative acts taken by the US government between 1933 and 1938. However, they represent only a small sample of the overall measures issued by the US government to regulate agriculture trade since then.

105 Ibid. (p. 45)

106 Ibid. (p. 46)

soil-conserving crops. The *Agricultural Marketing Agreement Act* of 1937 granted the US Department of Agriculture (USDA) the right to enact marketing agreements among producers in order to maintain 'orderly marketing conditions'. Prices were affected by the USDA's controls on quantity, quality and shipment rates. Lastly the *Agricultural Adjustment Act* of 1938 clarified the Soil Conservation and Domestic Allotment Act. The US government was mandated to establish quotas – with the approval of two-third of producers – for basic crops such as corn, wheat, cotton, rice, tobacco, and peanuts.[107]

These five acts form the backbone of the agricultural policy of the United States. To summarize, three basic mechanisms are used by the US government to control agricultural production: First, acreage limitation requirements or production cuts; second, government supported marketing agreement, either through government limits or through sanctioned producer agreements; and third price subsidization through direct payment, non recourse loans, or CCC purchases. These legislations have already established a policy of trade protectionism that aims at maintaining the farm incomes for agricultural products.

Last but not least, by the mid-1980s the United States, "a long-time critic of the EC export subsidies, began to enact export subsidies of its own. Among the first moves, in 1982 and 1983, were offers to low-interest loans to purchasers of American farm exports."[108] These initiatives were enacted and formalized in the 1985 US Farm Bill.[109] In order to reform her domestic support programmes, as required by the AoA in the framework of the Doha multilateral negotiations, the USA will have to play the game at two levels, domestic and international.

---

[107] Ibid. (p. 45f); Mahler (1991)

[108] Mahler (1991: 37)

[109] Ibid.

According to some trade experts, the collapse of global trade talks in July 2006 was due to domestic pressures put on the US President by his fellow citizens. For *Financial Express*, the unwillingness of the Bush's administration to risk alienating Farm Belt supporters with cuts in agricultural subsidies was the key factor in the collapse of talks in Geneva. With a Republican majority in Congress, President Bush did not want to dissatisfy his electorate. "Republicans hold 231 seats in the House of Representatives, where all 435 seats are up for re-election this year [2006], and 55 seats in the Senate, where a third of the 100 seats are being contested."[110] Bush needed the support of those farmers whose interests were represented in the Senate. Hence efforts to salvage trade talks on a global trade agreement felt victim to the difficult November mid-term election outlook that President Bush and his Republican Party faced in states where farm interests were highly represented. "Soybeans are Missouri, Iowa and Arkansas, among other Republican-voting states. Beef is Kansas, the Dakotas and the Solid South. Oranges are Florida."[111]

In June 2006, a bipartisan group of senators sent the White House a letter demanding a halt to further US farm concessions barring significant new overtures from Europe. According to Daniel Ikenson, a trade expert at the Cato Institute, a free-market think-tank based in Washington, "agricultural interests are very well represented in the Senate".[112] As Republicans feared they may loose elections in the Midwestern heartland, the Bush administration became even less willing to ask for additional sacrifices from American farmers. Judith Lee, an international trade lawyer in Washington, said that domestic politics had driven global trade talks from the beginning and that farm lobbies in the USA made it very difficult to put forward packages to move negotiations forward as politicians feared they were going to pay a price at the polls.[113] Political calculus at home and the fear to loose elections influenced the world trade agenda. The need to secure support at

---

[110] The Financial Express, 28 July 2006.

[111] Greider (2003)

[112] The Financial Express, 28 July 2006.

[113] Ibid.

home while trying to make deals at the international level made it difficult for the US President to influence the outcome of negotiations. Any move taken by President Bush at Level I that did not echo the views of domestic interest groups was blocked at Level II. The demands of domestic lobby groups do not always coincide with the concessions other international partners are ready to engage in.

At the international level, American farmers demanded reciprocity as condition *sine qua non* for cuts in export subsidies. Farm-state Republicans cheered the deadlock of trade negotiations and made it clear that "the United States is willing to change its domestic agriculture policies, but American farmers demand equal access to markets on the world stage".[114] For these farmers "no deal is better than a bad deal for America's producers."[115] Reciprocity seems to drive the move in agricultural trade talks. The Agriculture Agreement required that non-tariff barriers are converted into tariffs that should then be cut accordingly, in order to allow an unconditional market access to all members of the multilateral trading organization. In global trade talks however, the parties distrust one another when it comes to implement their commitments. Almost all American officials worry about the possibility of making concessions and not getting something in return. The US Agriculture Secretary Clayton Yeutter echoed this view and said that the US will "not accept cuts in subsidies, and in return, get nothing real in market access."[116] Also the US Trade Representative, ambassador Rob Portman followed suit: "The US proposal is offered in earnest", he noted. "We're ready to make meaningful changes to American farm programs provided our trading partners deliver tangible market access for U.S. agricultural exports and our offer is also met by substantial reductions in trade-distorting measures, with deeper cuts by the biggest subsidizers."[117] While Republican Senators need to preserve the farm interests of their domestic

---

[114] Ibid.
[115] Ibid.
[116] Ibid.
[117] USTR (2005b)

constituencies, they block, by the same token, agricultural reform expected at the international level.

In summary, US officials demand reciprocity as condition sine qua non for any change in their agricultural policy, while domestic groups want to preserve their farm interests. Could the EC do the first move and open its markets to American agricultural products?

### *3.2.2. The European Community*

The Common Agricultural Policy (CAP) of the EC was established by the Treaty of Rome (1957). This Treaty incorporated a carefully crafted compromise between the French and Germans, who were both determined to ensure that their domestic producers maintained the same advantages under the new Community-wide program that they had enjoyed under their respective national programs prior to the formation of the EC.[118] Title II of the *Consolidated Version of the Treaty Establishing the European Community*[119] is devoted to agriculture. Article 32 of the EC Treaty defines 'agricultural products' as products of the soil, of stock farming, of fisheries and products of first stage processing directly related to these products.[120] The early development of CAP was shaped by the recent memory of food rationing during World War II and the immediate post war period. According to Maria Margaronis, the much-reviled CAP came about partly as a result of the experience of famine during World War II. The Common Agricultural Policy of the EC "has its origins in the determination that Europe should never again see mass starvation. By protecting and supporting their farmers against the vagaries of trade while simultaneously investing in intensive agriculture [...], European governments hoped to insure long-term food security for their people."[121] Objectives of the CAP were to increase agricultural

---

118 Read Patterson (1997: 136)
119 Extract from Foster (2006: 1-103)
120 EC Treaty, Article 32.
121 Margaronis (1999)

productivity, to increase the individual earnings of persons working in agriculture, to stabilize markets, to safeguard supplies, and to insure that supply reach the consumer at reasonable prices.[122] However, attempts to maintain all these objectives simultaneously resulted in support programs that led to uncontrollable overproduction. For example, "between 1975 and 1986 the EC moved from being an overall net importer of agricultural produce [sic] to being a net exporter of cereals, sugar, wine, beef, and veal."[123] This increase in production affected the world agricultural market in two ways: First, European overproduction caused agricultural supplies to increase faster than demand. Second, to reduce stocks, the EC had to increase export subsidies. In so doing, non-EC exporters of agricultural commodities lost market share to the EC. It is under these circumstances that the EC stands in agricultural trade negotiations. For those foregoing reasons, different parties call for a radical reform of the CAP.

Contrary to the two-level games specific to other countries in international negotiations, the EC has to play three-level games in global trade talks. Policy reforms of CAP require negotiations at the domestic level (Level III), at the Community level (Level II), and at the international level (Level I). Negotiations at the three levels influence one another in different ways. Domestic coalitions affect the passage of Community agricultural policy and Community agricultural policy affects world markets; world market conditions both affect domestic coalitions and Community agricultural policy, so that the policy reform of the CAP presupposes a complicated system of negotiations that will occur simultaneously at several levels of the game. At both the international and EC levels, voices call for an overhaul reform of the CAP that absorbs more than 40 per cent of the EC budget.[124] While France is its stout defender, the United Kingdom is the aggressive attacker of the CAP at Level II.

---

122 Read EC Treaty, Art. 32-34.

123 Buckwell (1991), cited by Patterson (1997: 136)

124 Mehta (2005), modification of the CAP requires unanimous ratification by the Council of Ministers, representing each of the member states, read Putnam (1988: 449)

When Britain took over the EC presidency in July 2005, Tony Blair put a forceful case for reform of the CAP and more EC spending on science and research to the European Parliament. In his *Mansion House Speech* of November 2005, the former British Prime Minister focused his talks on trade negotiations of the WTO. As agriculture accounts only for about 2 per cent of the EC Gross Domestic Product (GDP) and roughly the same amount of employment, Tony Blair deplored the fact that rich-countries continue to use trade-distorting policies in the agricultural sector that deprive the hope of people living on less than $1 a day to escape out of extreme poverty: "Because everyone wants someone else to move first nobody has moved far enough and the talks seem to have stalled."[125] Echoing the voice of the General-Director of the WTO, Tony Blair said that the cutting of trade barriers by a third would boost the world economy by almost $600 billion. Gordon Brown, the former British Finance Minister,[126] followed suit and criticised the EC stubbornness to reform the CAP: "What better signal could Europe send of its commitment to wider economic reform than tackling wasteful subsidies that consume 40% of the European budget, even at time when agriculture accounts for just 2% of the European economy?"[127] This wave of criticisms of British officials was particularly directed against France that is considered a hard liner that opposes the CAP reform. This swipe at the French was responded by the former French President, Jacques Chirac, who demanded that until the British rebate was put on the negotiating table in Brussels, the CAP will not be subject to more radical reform.[128]

The British rebate was negotiated in 1984 at the Fontainebleu Conference by the former British Prime Minister, Mrs Thatcher. Uneasy about the level of French farming subsidies paid out through the CAP, she demanded 'I want my money back' and got it. Essentially, in any given year, British re-

---

[125] *Tony Blair's Mansion Speech*, in Guardian (2005a)

[126] Gordon Brown is British Prime Minister since 26 June 2007.

[127] Cited by Elliott (2005)

bate is equivalent to 66 per cent of the Britain's net contribution to the EC budget in the previous year.[129] When it was negotiated in 1984, Britain was the third poorest member of the community. It was so because Britain had fewer and more industrialized farms than France, and farm subsidies made up 70 per cent of EC expenditures. As a rule of thumb, the bigger the EC budget, the bigger the rebate. But the figure is usually between 2.7 billion and 3.2 billion pounds.[130] As 10 new member states joined the EC in May 2004, those nations, led by Poland, objected to a major handout being made to the second biggest contributor of the EC budget and the world's fourth-largest economy (Britain), while they were waiting for reconstruction funds. Britain's rebate is opposed by all other EC nations.[131] While those nations call for a freezing of the British rebate with the eventual aim of phasing it out altogether – a proposal brought by the Luxembourgian presidency – Britain pledges for more EC spending on science and research than on CAP. This row over the radical reform of CAP on the one side (Britain's proposal) and the freezing of the British rebate at the other side (other EC member states) reverberates on negotiations at both the domestic and international levels.

If the British rebate was to be frozen, Germany would probably have to agree to higher EC spending or cuts in aid to the former East Germany, France would have to accept cuts in rural subsidies, or agree to include Romania and Bulgaria in the farm budget once they join the EC in 2007, shrinking the pot for French farmers, so that in the end-game, everyone will have to suffer somewhere.[132]

At the domestic level, the former French President Jacques Chirac and former British Prime Minister Tony Blair had to face elections on May 2005: Blair's political survival depended on his Labour Party winning the elections

---

128 Ibid.
129 Guardian, the (2005c)
130 Ibid.
131 Helm and Rennie (2005a); Rennie (2005a)
132 Rennie (2005a)

scheduled for 5 May 2005; and Chirac needed a Yes vote for the European Constitution in a referendum on 29 May 2005.

During the EC summit in Brussels (March 2005), clashes between the two leaders became apparent. Chirac launched his attack – in response about the shape of the EC budget from 2007 to 2013 – during a press conference stating that "we can only truthfully achieve an appropriate balance if we re-open the debate on the British cheque [rebate]".[133] Jacques Chirac expected to glean some much needed kudos at home for grandstanding over Britain's rebate, what could help him win a Yes vote in France's referendum on the EC constitution. But the United Kingdom was also implacable when it came to defending 'her' rebate. Member of Parliament from the Conservative Party interpreted Chirac's comments as a sign that Tony Blair was not defending Britain's interests in Brussels. Having in mind that elections for the Lower House were to be held soon, a senior Conservative Member of Parliament said that the rebate was won by a Conservative government and that given Labour's record of surrender in EC negotiations, a Labour government could not keep the rebate that is crucial to Britain. The British government spokesman responded to both attacks in saying that the rebate was "fully justified in 1984 and is fully justified now [2005]. Even with it, Britain pays two and half times as much into the EU budget as France in absolute terms. Without it, it would be 14 times as much. There can be no deal on future financing in June [2005] that does not protect the rebate."[134] Speaking shortly before Mr Chirac attack, the British Foreign Secretary, promised to support the use of Britain's 'absolute veto' to protect the rebate, so did Gordon Brown.[135] The serious concern therefore was the linkage between the budget of the EC and the WTO trade talks of 2005 in Hong Kong. In the EC, negotiations at levels III and II impacted on trade talks at level I.

---

[133] Cited by Helm and Rennie (2005b)

[134] Ibid.

[135] Rennie (2005a); Helm and Rennie (2005b)

Although no agreement was reached at the Community level, the EC Trade Commissioner nevertheless made it clear to other international partners that the EC was prepared to phase out agricultural subsidies provided advanced developing countries such as India and Brazil make equivalent gestures: "We stand ready to flesh out our plans on agriculture and to negotiate for real improvements in market access to our markets for agricultural exporters, but this can only be done on the basis of fair reciprocity".[136] In a meeting with the civil society in New Delhi, India (2001), he further said: "We have seven million farmers in Europe to protect".[137] Responding to an intervention about the six hundred millions Indian farmers, the EC Trade Commissioner tersely said that it was the government of India who should take care of their interests.[138]

### *3.2.3. The G20*

The G20 is an informal coalition of countries that lacks a common agricultural policy. A study conducted by Anne Krueger, Maurice Schiff, and Aberto Valdés (1991) characterizes the policy mixes for 18 developing countries from 1960 to 1983 and classifies the agricultural policy of these 18 countries into different categories.[139] Four main categories of agricultural policy were depicted by the authors to whom member countries of the G20 also belong.

The first category includes major Southeast Asian countries such as Indonesia, Thailand, and China. The agrarian structure of these countries consisted predominantly of family farms, but they reduced agricultural taxation in the 1970s and started to support smallholders. For example, in 1978 "China abandoned collective agriculture; assigned most farm land to fami-

---

136 The Financial Express (2005a)

137 Mehta (2001)

138 Ibid.

139 Binswanger and Deininger (1997: 1961). The study included a large number of countries, but only member states of the G20 will be mentioned here.

lies, giving each a very small holding; and sharply increased the prices paid for agricultural goods."[140] Hence agricultural output of these countries grew rapidly, and the number of rural households living in poverty fell dramatically.

A second group of countries included Argentina, Nigeria, and Tanzania as well as other African countries that also had agrarian structures dominated by family farms. However, these countries discriminated against agricultural production by maintaining industrial protection and export taxation. They provided little support to farmers that went primarily to relatively inefficient, but politically powerful large producers. "Except in regions with especially favourable conditions, agricultural output has not kept up with population growth, and rural poverty has increased sharply."[141] These countries have started to reform agricultural policies to boost production in rural areas, but accompanying investment in public goods such as education, infrastructure, and basic science does not keep pace with the need to raise the living standards of these rural farmers.

A third group of countries including India, Mexico, and the Philippines, whose agrarian structures comprise large estates formed during colonial rule, also imposed heavy taxes on the agricultural sector through unfavourable policies such as an unsupportive regulatory environment, exchange rate restrictions, and import barriers. However, these countries implemented "large public investment programs in rural areas and partial land reform programs, which addressed structural problems."[142] This combination of policies resulted in modest increases in agricultural output and poverty reductions in rural areas.

---

140 Ibid. (p. 1962)

141 Ibid.

142 Ibid.

The fourth and last group of countries include Brazil, Guatemala, and South Africa that has been characterized by an unequal distribution of land (often with 2 per cent of farmers holding 33 per cent of the land).[143] This unequal distribution of land dates back to the colonial times and was worsened by a policy mix that taxed the agricultural sector directly and indirectly through industrial protection and overvalued exchange rates.

To sum up, the common denominator of the agricultural policies of the G20 prior to the 1980s is the following: First, most of the countries imposed direct and indirect taxes on their agricultural sector. Government-owned marketing boards were often established as the sole entity with the legal right to purchase, transport, and export agricultural products. Marketing boards set the price that farmers received for their crops:

> the difference between the price paid to domestic farmers at prices well bellow the world price represented a tax on agricultural incomes that the state could use to finance government-favoured projects in industry. [...] The trade barriers used to protect domestic manufacturing firms from foreign competition also represented a tax on the incomes of people working in agriculture.[144]

Direct taxes were implemented through government-owned marketing boards that controlled the purchase and export of agricultural commodities. Indirect taxation was levied through the imposition of high import tariffs on manufacturing products. Producers of agricultural goods, who were consumers rather than producers of these manufactured goods, therefore paid a much higher price for them than they would have in the absence of tariffs and quantitative restrictions.[145] Second, public investment in many developing countries focused on state-owned enterprises and large-scale agriculture, in which state involvement may crowd out private investment. Such

---

143 Ibid.

144 Oatley (2004: 139)

145 In Brazil and Colombia for instance, governments taxed coffee exports; the government of Thailand taxed rubber and rice exports. See Oatley (2004: 139)

government policies transferred income from rural agriculture to the urban manufacturing sector. And finally, land reforms in developing countries privileged large farmers having political clout while the ownership of land also remained highly concentrated.[146] From the 1980s onward however, the agricultural policy of these countries slightly changed and their governments started to encourage the export-competing agricultural sector, although many of the big farms remain state-owned properties.

In agricultural trade negotiations, the interests of the G20 converge more towards a radical liberalization of agricultural trade and less towards the liberalization of manufactured products. The G20 emerged in 2003 under special circumstances that are worth mentioning here.

After the fourth session of the WTO Ministerial Conference in Doha (2001), agriculture negotiations were blocked for months by disagreement between the USA and the EC regarding which formula to use for tariff reductions in agricultural products. On one of the boards, the USA preferred a Swiss formula (cutting high tariffs more than lower tariffs), while on the other board the EC – reluctant to reduce its high tariffs in sensitive sectors such as dairy, sugar and meat – preferred a Uruguay Round formula (cutting tariff by the same percentage). The USA and the EC finally released a 'framework' agreement incorporating both their interests on 13 August 2003. This suggested a 'blended' tariff formula that the developing world did not like.[147] As the Cairns Group made no effective response to the USA/EC framework agreement, an informal coalition of countries submitted a joint response on 20 August 2003: this marked the birth of the G20.

---

146 The initial land allocations of the United States and Brazil in the late nineteenth century are illustrative here. In the USA, the Homesteading Acts limited the size of plots that families could acquire to 160 acres. United States agriculture became one of the most productive systems in the world. By contrast, most of Brazil land could be titled only in lots no smaller than four squares kilometres (988 acres) – an area much larger than a family could work, see Biswanger and Deininger (1997: 1967)

147 Jawara and Kwa (2004: XXVI). Under the blended formula, a proportion of tariff lines would be cut by a fixed percentage and the bulk by a Swiss formula, and some to zero or near zero.

From August 2003 on, the USA, the EC and the G20 stand at the forefront of agricultural trade negotiations. According to Elliott and Denny (2003), the emergence of the G20 changed the dynamic of trade talks: "where once the EU and the US had ruled the roost, they were now confronted with an alliance of more than 20 countries representing most of the world's population and most of its fastest-growing economies." In the global trade talks, demands of the G20 are threefold: First, the group pledges for better access to the US and EC markets for their agricultural products; second the group demands a new deal for cotton farmers, particularly in West Africa, and third it wants to exclude new issues from the Doha Agenda.[148] Demands of the G20 contradict with those of the USA and the EC. While the G20 wants deeper cuts in import barriers of the developed countries, caps on all rich-country farm payments and an end to the subsidies on exported food that let cheap US and EC products flood global markets; the USA wants concessions from the G20 in return for reducing trade barriers; and the EC wants trade to delve into the four new issues of investment, competition, government procurement and trade facilitation. Regarding the demands of the G20, the US Trade Representative said that his government was ready to concede changes in its agricultural policy if full reciprocity was obtained. The EC was still divided on this issue. While Britain proposed more concessions, the EC agricultural trade commissioner adopted a rather cautious approach.

Britain's trade secretary Patricia Hewitt and agriculture secretary, Margaret Beckett were of the view that rich-countries should make trade work for the poor, while the EC trade agriculture commissioner, Franz Fischler, was of the view that the EC should strongly defend its farmers. Britain believed that a deal to cut farm subsidies in rich countries is the key to developing support for a new global trade deal. Ms Hewitt made it clear that her government saw reforms of the CAP as a good basis for negotiations with the

---

[148] Elliott and Denny (2003)

G20: "Rich countries can't preach free trade abroad and have protectionism at home. There is a danger of locking developing countries into poverty because we lock them out of our markets"[149], she said. To compound the problem, the British government framed its priority to a better deal for the G20 and other developing countries, whilst hinting at the difficulty to agree with other EC member states. Predicting a possible collapse of the global trade talks, Ms Hewitt dubbed such a failure a disaster for the global economic stability. "If we fail it will be a disaster for the world economy", and continued "we will have failed to give a boost to confidence, failed to offer a real prospect of moving people out of poverty and failed to provide an economy to underpin the coalition against terrorism we've been trying to construct since 9/11."[150] Britain's trade secretary pledged for more actions from rich countries to broker a deal in trade talks that will give a boost to the world economy, but also improve the support to fight international terrorism.

In response to this appeal, the EC agriculture commissioner said that developing countries demanded that developed countries make drastic changes, while they themselves did nothing. "If I look at the recent extreme proposal co-sponsored by Brazil, China, India and others, I cannot help [getting] the impression that they are circling in a different orbit," Mr Fischler said, "If they want to do business, they should come back to mother earth. If they choose to continue their space odyssey they will not get the stars, they will not get the moon, they will end up with empty hands."[151] Widening the scope of his response to the critics of the CAP, he also accused non-governmental organizations, which frequently claim that CAP damages the market share of developing countries. He made it clear that the EC did not believe all developing countries deserved major concessions because , as he noted, some were really poor, but others were net food exporters and far more prosperous. The EC trade commissioner followed suit, pointing out that 70 per cent of customs duties paid on goods exported from the devel-

---

149 Cited by Osborn and Elliott (2003)

150 Cited by Mathiason (2003)

oping world were levied by other developing countries.[152] However, the G20 had its own ideas about what should emerge from global trade talks, and they appeared radically different from the US and EC's blueprint.

During the Cancún Ministerial Conference of 2003, a last-ditch concession from the EC trade commissioner on investment and competition, the most controversial issues, failed to appease developing countries. But when Japan and Korea declared that they were also holding out for all the four issues, the chairman of the meeting, the Mexican foreign secretary, Mr Luis Ernesto Derbez ended the talks and the Cancún Ministerial came to a halt. In response to the British and other ministers critiques of this abrupt halt of the meeting, Mr Derbez said: "I don't think I made a rash decision, I think I made a rational decision... Consensus was not there and there was no way to build it."[153] The balance of power at the WTO has shifted for good, what made Elliott and Denny to conclude that, in the end, it was the poorest and least powerful countries that brought negotiations to a halt. The failure at Cancún was differently perceived. The G20 went on the offensive with a declaration of the Brazilian foreign minister, stating that "the G20 will continue to play a decisive role in agricultural negotiations."[154] The USA and the EC took different views on how to react to the flexing of muscles by the developing world. Washington dropped a less than subtle hint that it is considering turning its back on the multilateral trading system in favour of bilateral deals with friendly countries. By contrast, The EC trade commissioner declared he would leave his last minute concessions from Cancún on the table when negotiations restart.[155]

The failure of the Cancún Ministerial Conference prompted the different parties to soften their different positions, if they wanted the multilateral trading

---

151 Cited by Osborn and Elliott (2003)

152 Ibid.

153 Cited by Elliott and Denny (2003)

154 Ibid.

system to survive. In July 2004, a deal was made that tried to incorporate the demands of the different parties. The text that came out of negotiations is referred to as 'the July Package'. The next chapter is devoted to the content of this text.

[155] Ibid.

# 4. Outcome of Negotiations

After years of intense negotiations between the USA, the EC and the G20, the General Council[156] of the WTO adopted a post-Cancún decision on 1 August 2004 for the revival of trade talks. The text of this decision is referred to as the 'July 2004 Package' or shortly called, the 'July Package'.

## 4.1. The July Package

The July Package deals with issues such as agriculture, non-agricultural market access, development, services, other negotiating bodies, trade facilitation, and other elements of the work. Four annexes, A, B, C, and D are hung upon the text. Annex A is devoted to agriculture and cotton; annex B to non-agricultural market access and development issues; annex C to trade in services and other negotiation bodies; and annex D to the new issue of trade facilitation. This section will concentrate only on those paragraphs that deal with agricultural trade and the negotiating modalities, as set out in Annex A of the document.

The 'July Package' was mainly tailored to the developing countries' needs and demands. The General Council acknowledged the central role agriculture plays for the economic development of poor countries.[157] The Council also recognised the importance of cotton for some West African countries.[158] Due to this, a subcommittee on cotton was established that meets periodically and reports to the Special Session of the Committee on Agriculture. The work of the cotton subcommittee encompasses all trade-distorting policies affecting the sector in all three pillars of market access, domestic

---

156 The General Council is the main body of the WTO where all member states are permanently represented.

157 WT/L/579, Annex A (para. 2)

158 Ibid (para. 4)

support, and export competition.[159] The General Council instructed the Secretariat to continue to work with the development community and to provide the Council with periodic reports on relevant matters of interest to these countries. Furthermore, the Council reasserted that the fuller integration of small, vulnerable economies into the multilateral trading system should be addressed, without creating a sub-category of members, as mandated in Paragraph 35 of the Doha Ministerial Declaration. One of the sweeping reforms introduced by the Council was the exclusion of three of the four new issues, trade and investment, trade and competition, and transparency in government procurement, from the Doha Ministerial Declaration, mentioned in paragraphs 20 to 22, 23 to 25 and 26 respectively.[160] From the four new issues, only 'trade facilitation' was recognised as an integral part of the Doha Work Programme.

In general, the text of the July Package simply readjusted some provisions of the Doha Ministerial Declaration and reaffirmed, with a view to correct, some provisions of the Agriculture Agreement. Therefore, the three pillars of agricultural trade liberalization came once more under scrutiny.

Concerning the *domestic support commitments*, Special and Differential Treatment were recognised as an integral component of negotiations. As stated in the Agriculture Agreement, developing countries were granted longer implementation periods, and least developed countries did not have to make any commitments. Higher levels of permitted trade-distorting domestic support were subject to proportional higher cuts. A 'tiered formula' was adopted for this purpose. Under this formula, members having higher levels of trade-distorting domestic support had to make greater overall reductions in order to achieve harmonizing results. In the first year and throughout the implementation period, the sum of all trade-distorting sup-

---

159 Initiated by the WTO Secretariat itself, a workshop on cotton was organized in Cotonou (Benin) from 23 to 24 March 2004 that ushered in this new initiative.

160 WT/L/579, Annex A (g)

port should not exceed 80 per cent of the sum of the Final Bound Total AMS. Additionally, reductions in *de minimis* were to be negotiated taking into account the principle of SDT. Developing countries that allocate almost all *de minimis* to support subsistence and resource-poor farmers were exempted from reductions.[161] The General Council also recognised the role of the 'blue box' in promoting agricultural reforms. Hence, direct payments under production-limiting programmes were allowed. However, blue box support should not exceed 5 per cent of the member average total value of agricultural production during an historical period that was to be established in the negotiations.[162]

Regarding the pillar of *export competition*, member states agreed to establish detailed modalities ensuring parallel elimination of all forms of export subsidies. The General Council enhanced some recommendations of the Doha Ministerial Declaration for "reduction of, with a view to phasing out, all forms of export subsidies."[163] The following subsidies were to be eliminated by the end date to be agreed: export subsidies, export credits, export credit guarantees or insurance programmes; terms and conditions relating to export credits; trade distorting practices; provision of food aid that is not in conformity with operationally effective disciplines to be agreed.[164] However, developing countries had to benefit from longer implementation periods for the phasing out of all forms of export subsidies. Members should ensure that the disciplines on export credits, export credit guarantees or insurance programs to be agreed make appropriate provision for differential treatment in favour of net food-importing developing countries. In exceptional circumstances, which could not be covered by food aid, export credits or preferential international financing facilities, ad hoc temporary measures relating to exports to developing countries may be agreed by the members.[165]

---

161 Ibid. (para. 11)
162 Ibid. (para. 13-15)
163 WT/MIN(01)/DEC/1 (para. 13)
164 WT/L/579, Annex A (para. 18)
165 Ibid. (para. 26)

Concerning the last pillar of *market access*, the Doha Ministerial Declaration also calls for "substantial improvements in market access."[166] Members agreed that SDT for developing countries members would be an integral part of negotiations. They also agreed that tariff reductions would take into account the different tariff structures of developed and developing countries' members. Each member state was allowed to designate a list of 'Sensitive Products' that requires flexibility in tariff cuts. "Members may designate an appropriate number, to be negotiated, of tariff lines to be treated as sensitive, taking account of existing commitments for these products."[167] In addition to these sensitive products, developing countries members were given the flexibility to designate an appropriate number of products as 'Special Products', based on criteria of food security, livelihood security and rural development needs. These products should be eligible for more flexible treatment as well.[168] SDT for developing countries were once again reasserted as an integral part of all elements of negotiation, including the tariff reduction formula, the number and treatment of sensitive products, the expansion of tariff rate quota, and the implementation period.

In summary, the July Package introduced three novelties in the Doha Agenda: First, of the four highly divisive new issues, only trade facilitation was recognised as an integral part of the Doha Work Programme. Trade and investment, trade and competition, and transparency in government procurement were, altogether, excluded from the agenda. Second, a subcommittee on cotton was established that meets periodically and reports to the Special Session of the Committee on Agriculture. In doing so, the concerns of some West African countries, whose economies almost entirely depend on cotton industry, were met. Third, a 'tiered formula' was adopted

---

166 WT/MIN(01)/DEC/1 (para. 13)

167 WT/L/579, Annex A (para. 31)

168 Ibid. (para. 41)

for cuts in agricultural subsidies, so that countries with high subsidies had also to accept deeper cuts.

Like the Agriculture Agreement, the July Package was an agreement made at Level I. However, the difficulty to liberalize agricultural trade is not linked to the inability of member states of the multilateral trading system to make agreements at Level I, the stalemate stems from the failure to implement these agreements at the domestic level.

## 4. 2. Implementation-Related Concerns

The liberalization of agricultural trade is differently perceived by domestic constituencies. During the negotiations, different farmers oppose, or push for, the liberalization of agricultural trade. On a protest march against the WTO Ministerial Conference in Cancún, 2003, a South Korean farmer committed suicide while a peasant resistance group, the Zapatistas, based in the southern Mexican state of Chiapas, seized control of the state-owned radio station to protest against the US and EC farm policies.[169] In 2005, Parliamentarians of the Britain's Conservative Party warned British Prime Minister not to surrender the British rebate in agricultural trade negotiations in Brussels. In June 2006, a bipartisan group of Senators sent a letter to the White House demanding a halt to further US concessions on agricultural liberalization. In India, farmers warned their government to strongly represent their interests in agricultural trade negotiations. With 65 per cent of the Indian population working in the agricultural sector,[170] the country heavily depends on agricultural exports to boost its economy. All these protests attest how sensitive agricultural trade negotiations are. One thing is to make agreements at Level I and the other to convince domestic interest groups for their ratification.

---

169 Denny and Elliott (2003)
170 Mehta (2001)

Kim and Smith distinguish between the making of agreement and their enforcement in the process of trade liberalization: "When we describe the processes of trade liberalization, we need to distinguish between making agreements and maintaining (or enforcing) agreements."[171] No matter how difficult it might be to make agreements at the international level, if those agreements cannot be implemented, maintained and enforced at the domestic level, they are going to be less useful in moving the system toward greater openness. Once an agreement is made at the international level, international negotiators must convince their domestic constituencies for ratification. Two policy options are possible: the adherence to the agreement or the defection from it. If all countries adhere to the agreement, a collective action is achieved and public good – in this case, agricultural trade liberalization – is provided. If some adhere and others do not, or no party adhere to the agreement at all, a collective action problem arises.

### *4.2.1. Provision of the Public Good: A Collective Action Problem*

States must implement, maintain and enforce agreements, in order for multilateral negotiations to move the system toward the provision of the public good. A public good involves the qualities of *non-excludability* and *joint supply*. Non excludability means that once a good has been provided, there is no way to prevent non-contributors from consuming it. Joint supply refers to the existence of non rivalry in the consumption of the good; as such consumption does not diminish the quantity or quality of the benefit available to other states.[172] Olson's well-known treatment of the provision of collective

---

171 Kim and Smith (1997: 433f)

172 Snidal (1985: 929); Conybeare (1984: 6f). Conybeare doubts whether free trade is typically a public good problem. He bases his assumption on empirical facts that free trade exhibits excludability and rivalry. This assumption only holds if one considers free trade to take place outside a multilateral framework, like he does. However, the WTO is based on an unconditional MFN clause, what *de jure* makes the public good consumable to all the member states.

goods[173] argues that "*the larger the group, the farther it will fall short of providing an optimal amount of a collective good.*"[174] He provides three reasons why the size of the group matters in its inability to provide a collective good: First, the fraction of the group benefit received by any one individual declines as the size increases; second, larger groups are less likely to exhibit small-group strategic interaction that could help in collective good provision; and finally, organizational costs increase with an increase in group size.[175]

Applied to agricultural trade liberalization, however, the first proposition about the decrease of individual benefits as the group size increases does not hold. According to the World Bank, if all the parties were to enforce the agreements made so far in knocking down barriers to trade in agricultural goods, services and intellectual property rights, at least $96 billion could be pumped into the global economy,[176] and all members of the WTO could profit from them. Each member of the WTO has a stake in at least one area of trade negotiations in the Doha round. Thus, as the WTO membership increases, so will the trade outlet and the gains received by each member, all other things being equal.

The second proposition regarding the inability of large group to exhibit small-group strategic interaction can be explained as follows: In smaller groups, individuals' contributions will be larger, and as a result their probabilities of deciding the outcome will be larger as well. Conversely, when the group is too large, individual contribution to the provision of the public good will tend to be small, and as a result the probability of each individual to decide on the outcome will tend to be small as well – so small, perhaps, as to make the expected benefits of a contribution negligible.[177] Therefore,

---

173 Public and collective goods are used here as synonyms.
174 Olson (1968: 35), the original text is emphasised.
175 Ibid. (p. 48)
176 The Financial Express (2007a)
177 Read Alt and Gilligan, in Frieden and Lake (2004: 329); Conybeare (1984: 6)

small groups will strongly exhibit strategic interaction that could help in collective good provision than large groups.

Olson's last proposition about the increase of organizational costs as the group size increases is also problematic, when it is analysed in the context of an international organization (WTO). The aim of international organizations is to reduce organizational costs, to transmit considerable information, increase transparency, reduce uncertainty, and help to inspire confidence among treaty parties.[178] Hence the increase in group size does not influence organizational costs once an iterated discourse and rules of the game are institutionalized.

States prefer liberalization that is based on reciprocity, and reciprocity is the "*exchanges of roughly equivalent values in which the actions of each party are contingent on the prior actions of the others in such a way that good is returned for good, and bad for bad.*"[179] The exchanges of values are often, but not always, mutually beneficial; they must be based on self-interest, as well as, on shared understanding of rights and obligations; and the value of what is exchanged may or may not be comparable. In respect to agricultural trade liberalization, reciprocity means that the USA is only willing to cut her tariffs if she is certain that the EC and the G20 will do the same. And the cuts must be roughly equivalent, which as in the case of agriculture will not pose a big problem, as the Agriculture Agreement itself is explicit about such cuts. Interesting however, is the notion of contingency of actions among interested parties. This notion presupposes that actions of each party are conditional to the prior actions of the others. Clearly stated, reciprocity means that, if the G20 enforces its commitments, the USA may be willing to do the same and the EC, as well. On the contrary, if the G20 reneges on its commitments, the other parties will respond by reneging on the own commitments as well. Axelrod (1981) dubs such strategies Tit for Tat

---

178 Alvarez (2002: 147)

179 Keohane (1986: 8). The quotation is emphasised in the original text.

policies. "TIT FOR TAT is the policy of cooperating on the first move and then doing whatever the other player did on the previous move. This means that TIT FOR TAT will defect once for each defection by the other player."[180] When players are using Tit for Tat, a player who always defects will receive defection in return, and a player who cooperates is met with cooperation provided that the game is iterated. Therefore, with reciprocity parties are ready to return good for good and bad for bad. On closer look, reciprocity has two quite distinct meanings: *specific reciprocity* is distinct from *diffuse reciprocity*.

Specific reciprocity refers to situations "in which specified partners exchange items of equivalent value in a strictly delimited sequence. If any obligations exist, they are clearly specified in terms of rights and duties of particular actors."[181] Items of equivalent value and the partners who exchange them are specified in the case of specific reciprocity. In situations characterized by diffuse reciprocity however, the definition of equivalence is not precise, and obligations are more important. "Diffuse reciprocity involves conforming to generally accepted standards of behaviour."[182] Specific reciprocity requires bilateral balancing between particular actors; diffuse reciprocity emphasises an overall balance within a group. So, specific reciprocity reflects the concept of conditional MFN treatment, while diffuse reciprocity embodies unconditional MFN treatment. For an illustration, an unconditional MFN clause obliges a country not to discriminate against any other country with which it has an agreement. If A and B have a reciprocal trade agreement, and A makes a new agreement with C, concessions made by A to C are also applicable to B automatically. However, under conditional MFN clause, B will only receive those concessions, if it provides 'equivalent' compensation to A.[183] The concept of reciprocity has a core meaning and thus

---

180 Axelrod (1981: 308)

181 Keohane (1986: 4)

182 Ibid.

183 The multilateral trading system functions on the basis of an unconditional MFN clause.

can be defined in a way that is consistent with both the notion of specific and diffuse reciprocity. Two essential dimensions of the concept are noteworthy, namely *contingency* and *equivalence*.

First, reciprocal behaviour implies contingency because it requires interacting partners to return ill for ill and good for good. Actors who behave in a reciprocal fashion respond to cooperation with cooperation and to defection with defection. Second, equivalence is a rather complicated concept as it is impossible to precisely measure equivalence of benefits. In the absence of precise measurement, reciprocity will at least mean rough equivalent benefits.[184] In agricultural trade negotiations, the problem of equivalence was solved through SDT between the developing and developed world. Member countries of the G20 do not have to cut their tariffs as high as the USA and the EC. Additionally, the G20 is granted longer implementation periods than the other two parties. However, the cuts of the three groups of countries are considered to be roughly equivalent depending on their levels of economic development.

As the world trading system is based on an unconditional MFN clause, the granting of a privilege to one member state will automatically be extended to third states, irrespective of whether such third countries reciprocate by granting the same kinds of privileges in return. This situation creates a certain 'game' between negotiating partners, which can be better analysed using the prisoner's dilemma.

### *4.2.2. Enforcement of Agreements: A Prisoner's Dilemma*

The prisoner's dilemma is a story in which two individuals are accused of robbery. But the prosecutor or district attorney does not have sufficient evidence to condemn both of them, unless, at least one of the suspects reveals additional information to him/her. Nevertheless, he/she has evidence

---

[184] Keohane (1986: 8)

to convict both of them of a lesser crime, for instance because of carrying a firearm without permission. The two suspects are placed in different interrogation rooms. The prosecutor tells each prisoner that, in case one of them confesses and reveals the truth, he/she will get a much lighter sentence. If both prisoners confess, however, they each get heavier sentence than if they both remain silent and are charged with the lesser crime. Confessing to the prosecutor could bring the minimal sentence to one of the suspects if the other remains silent but could also lead to a heavier sentence if the other also confesses, in which case the prosecutor has the evidence to condemn both on more serious offences. Thus, the suspects are faced with two alternatives, either to remain silent or to confess. Remaining silent may lead to either a moderate sanction, if the other suspect remains silent as well, or the maximum penalty if the other one speaks to the attorney. Facing this situation and unable to communicate, the logical strategy for both prisoners is to choose to confess.

The prisoner's dilemma game has been applied to problems of international cooperation by different authors.[185] In Table 1 below, the two prisoners are represented by **States A** and **B** and policy alternatives are indicated by **0** and **1,** where **0** represents 'Cooperation' and **1** 'Defection' for each of the states. The entries in each cell represents ordinal pay offs for **States A** and **B**, respectively. The ordinal payoffs run from **4**, that is, the 'Most Preferred Outcome' to **1**, which is the 'Least preferred Outcome'. The prisoner's dilemma game reproduced here is a two-two matrix game with two states and two options. If **State A** and **State B** cooperate, both will get their best outcome (payoffs **3, 3**); if **State A** cooperates while **State B** defects, **A** will get its worst outcome **1** and **B** its best outcome **4**. If **B** cooperates while **A** defects the outcome will be reversed, **B** will end up with its worst outcome **1** and **A** with the best outcome **4**. However, if both state defect, they both get the payoffs **2** and **2**.

---

185 See Snidal (1985). Applied to problems of international cooperation, the prisoners are replaced by states that act as individual actors.

<u>Table 1</u>: **Prisoner's Dilemma**

| | | State B | |
|---|---|---|---|
| | | **0** | **1** |
| **State A** | **0** | **3, 3** | **1, 4** |
| | **1** | **4, 1** | **2, 2** |

Source: *Snidal (1985:927)*

For **State A**, the best payoff will be **4, 1** > **3, 3** > **2, 2** > **1, 4**; and for **State B**, the best outcome will be **1, 4** > **3, 3** > **2, 2** > **4, 1**, where '>' means 'superior to'. Acting as self-interested actors, both states will choose options that give them the highest utility. The pursuit of individual self-interests – represented by the dominant strategy **1** – results in the payoff (**2, 2**), which is the third best outcome for both states. Cooperation – represented by their choice of strategy **0** – could make both states better off. However, the dilemma persists even if cooperation is achieved, because both states will continue to have strong incentives to defect and the system is likely to return to the stable non-cooperative and deficient equilibrium represented by the outcome (**2, 2**).

Applied to agricultural trade liberalization, the prisoner's dilemma offers some important insights into what may cause the stalemate. By replacing the policy strategy **0** with '**Liberalize**' and strategy **1** with '**Protect**', the prisoner's dilemma looks as follows:

**Table 2: Prisoner's Dilemma and Trade Liberalization**

| | | State B | |
|---|---|---|---|
| | | **Liberalize** | **Protect** |
| **State A** | **Liberalize** | **l, l** | **l, p** |
| | **Protect** | **p, l** | **p, p** |

Source: *Adapted from Oatley (2004: 45)*

The preference orders of **State A** will be **p, l** > **l, l** > **p, p** > **l, p** and for **State B** the orders will be **l, p** > **l, l** > **p, p** > **p, l.** Defection from the agreement could bring higher payoffs to the one party, provided that the other cooperates. Each state therefore is aware of the fact that it could improve its payoffs if it defects and worsens it if it cooperates, while the other defects. Hence, the most secured position for both states is defection, that is, **Protection**. Both parties will end up protecting although cooperation yields higher payoffs. The *protect/protect* outcome is the *Nash Equilibrium*.

A Nash Equilibrium is an outcome at which neither player has an incentive to change strategies unilaterally, that is, an outcome in which none of the players can improve his or her situation by changing their individual strategy.[186] If **State A** unilaterally changes its strategy from *protect* to *liberalize*, the outcome shifts to *liberalize/protect*, the **State A's** least preferred outcome. Thus **State A** has no incentive to change its strategy unilaterally. By the same token, if **State B** changes its strategy from *protect* to *liberalize*, the outcome become *protect/liberalize*, **State B's** least preferred outcome. Hence **State B** has no motivation to change its strategy unilaterally either. The prisoner's dilemma's conclusion is that, even though **State A** and **State B** know that they will gain from trade liberalization, neither has the incentive to liberalize unilaterally. The *protect/protect* outcome is Pareto sub-optimal because both states can realise higher payoffs at *liberalize/liberalize*.

An outcome is *Pareto optimal* when no single actor can be made better off, without at the same time making another actor worse off.[187] The only way for both states to improve their pay offs without making each other worse off is to play the *liberalize/liberalize* strategy. However, the *protect/protect* outcome is the dominant strategy, although it produces a Pareto sub-optimal outcome and makes both states poorer than they would be if both liberalize trade.

Applied to the current negotiations on agricultural trade liberalization, a two-by-two matrix of the prisoner's dilemma game described so far is rather limited. The game normally requires that the parties cannot communicate, they cannot change their action once it is taken, and it assumes that there is only a one-shot play, so that the incentives to initiate cooperation is near to nil. None of these conditions can be satisfied in the real world of trade negotiations. In real world situations, states can communicate and change their actions; they can wait for the other to move first and the game can be iterated. Thus, the two-by-two prisoner's dilemma fails to take into account three variables constitutive of agricultural trade negotiations: First, there are large numbers of states[188] engaged in negotiations than only two; second, the game is iterated so that players can communicate. Axelrod (1981) has elaborated on this point by showing that a cooperative tit-for-tat strategy can dominate a dynamic prisoner's dilemma game if the players do not discount future gains too heavily. Therefore, tit-for-tat can yield more Pareto optimal outcomes where reciprocity has been institutionalized. Third, available policy choices in agricultural trade liberalization are more complex and multidimensional. Policy choices range from a Pareto optimal outcome (**3, 3**) to a Pareto sub-optimal outcome (**2, 2**) with a full array of intermediate

---

[186] Oatley (2004: 47); Aggarwal and Dupont, in Ravenhill (2005: 35)

[187] Oatley (2004: 47)

[188] On prisoner's dilemma game with large numbers, read Hardin (1968); Hardin (1971)

policy options in-between. Such intermediate policy choices are depicted in Table 3 below.

**Table 3: Graduated Prisoner's Dilemma**[189]

| | | State A | | | | |
|---|---|---|---|---|---|---|
| | | .0<br>K | .25 | .5<br>L | .75 | 1.0 |
| State B | .0 | 3.0, 3.0 | 2.5, 3.3 | 2.0, 3.5 | 1.5, 3.8 | 1.0, 4.0 |
| | .25 | 3.3, 2.5 | 2.8, 2.8 | 2.3, 3.0 | 1.8, 3.3 | 1.3, 3.5 |
| | .5 J | 3.5, 2.0 | 3.0, 2.3 | 2.5, 2.5 | 2.0, 2.8 | 1.5, 3.0 |
| | .75 | 3.8, 1.5 | 3.3, 1.8 | 2.8, 2.0 | 2.3, 2.3 | 1.8, 2.5 |
| | 1.0 | 4.0, 1.0 | 3.5, 1.3 | 3.0, 1.5 | 2.5, 1.8 | 2.0, 2.0 |

Source: *Snidal (1985: 928)*

Although the basic structure of the game remains the same when intermediate policy choices are introduced, the game is altered in two important ways. First, in the simple game, there is a single Pareto efficient outcome at the top left hand corner (**3, 3**). In the graduated game, there is a larger set of available cooperative and Pareto-efficient outcomes, as represented by the dark line segment **JKL** of Table 3. Although cooperation at (**3, 3**) is the best payoff for both states, there still exist a possibility to bargain for a better outcome along **JKL**. Second, the graduated games allow states to achieve intermediate levels of cooperation in circumstances where they are unwilling to risk complete cooperation. As this will be shown below, countries do not completely discount the commitments taken at Level I; they rather look for alternative ways for their partial implementation. Therefore, they opt for intermediate policies such as non-tariff barriers where bound tariffs are required, they classify their domestic support programmes into

189 Numerical entries should be treated as indicating only ordinal preferences where, for example, the outcome **3.5** is preferred to **3.25**.

blue boxes and/or green boxes to justify their support programmes, and they use technical barriers to trade and other red tapes to circumvent their WTO obligations. These measures cannot be classified as full cooperation or complete defection either; they are seen as intermediate policies located in-between the Pareto optimal outcome and the Nash equilibrium in a graduated prisoner's dilemma game.

Chapter 5 will ascertain whether such intermediate policies are indeed chosen by the different parties to negotiations.

# 5. Agricultural Policy Reforms

This chapter deals with the agricultural policy reforms of the USA, the EC and their impact on the G20 farming. The pattern of negotiations depicted so far between the three groups of countries exhibits the following features: the G20 protects its non agricultural sectors, in which the USA and the EC have a comparative advantage. Conversely, both the USA and the EC protect the agricultural sector where the G20 could be better off, if all trade-distorting policies were phased out. Thus, as far as, agricultural trade liberalization is concerned, the G20 stands as a plaintiff, the USA and the EC as the defendants.[190] Clearly stated, the G20 complains about the problem of 'predatory income transfers' in agricultural trade. A predatory income transfer is a form of rent-seeking that involves the usage of state power to transfer rather than create wealth.[191] By protecting their domestic markets and subsidizing their domestic farmers, the USA and the EC deter the G20's entry into world markets. This allows the US and EC farmers/ processors to have big shares on those markets. Cotton in the USA and sugar in the EC serve as case studies here.

The selection of cotton and sugar as case studies is based on methodological grounds. An 'extreme case' design was chosen in order to get as much information as possible about the level of subsidies paid to US and EC farmers respectively. As William James noted, moments of extremity often reveal the essence of a situation: "Consider cases A, B, C, D, E, F, and G, which vary along dimension X. Let us say that A, B, C, D, E, and F, vary minimally, whereas G exemplifies an extreme value (either 'positive' or 'negative'). Ceteris paribus, G will be the most useful case for in-depth

---

[190] The dichotomy plaintiff versus defendant could be reversed if this study rather focused on services, or intellectual property rights. In these sectors, the USA and EC could stand as plaintiffs and the G20 as defendant. Moreover, the non-agricultural sector is not part of this analysis.

[191] Conybeare (1984: 8)

analysis."[192] By replacing the above-mentioned alphabetic letters A, B, C, D, E, F and G with different crops in the USA and EC that vary along one dimension X (level of subsidies received), G will stand for cotton in the USA and for sugar in the EC, two crops that exemplify high levels of subsidization and hence, useful for an in-depth study of trade distorting policies. Since one cannot accurately measure the degree of trade-distorting policies, it was deemed appropriate to look to the most extreme cases of this phenomenon, namely cotton in the USA and the sugar in the EC in order to find out what trade-distorting policy means or can mean.

The level of subsidies paid to cotton and sugar beet growers as well as to their first stage processors will be simultaneously analysed in this chapter. Although cotton and sugar have undergone some first stage processing, they nevertheless remain agricultural products.[193] Different reasons can explain the mixture of both sectors 'agriculture' and 'first stage processing firm' here: First, cotton must be harvested from the cotton plant and transformed into a silky soft fibre, tradable cotton; and sugar beet or cane sugar must be processed in order to obtain raw sugar traded on world markets. Second, in the EC, sugar beet growers depend on the quota allocated to them by processors who in turn depend on national government allocations.[194] Furthermore, co-operatives of sugar beet growers have controlling stakes in processing industries such as Nordzucker and Sudzucker in Germany.[195] This 'vertical integration' between sugar beet growers and corporate processing industries make it difficult not to include the processing sector when analysing the agricultural policy of the EC. Finally, small-scale farming does not significantly influence domestic politics in the USA and the EC like the large-scale farming, first stage processing industries do. Thus,

---

[192] Gerring (2001: 217)

[193] The EC for instance defines agricultural products as "products of the soil and products of *first stage processing* directly related to these products", read the EC Treaty, Article 32.

[194] Oxfam (2004a: 19)

[195] Ibid. (p. 20)

an attempt to inquire why the ratification process of agricultural agreements is blocked at the domestic level must also take into account the interests of agricultural processors.

## 5.1. United States: Cotton Regime Reform?

When signing the Farm Bill in May 2002, US President George Bush made the following remarks:

> I told the people, I said if you give me a chance to be the President, we're not going to treat our agricultural industry as a secondary citizen when it comes to opening up markets. And I mean that .... The farm bill is important legislation.... It will improve farmer independence, and preserve the farm way of life. It helps America's farmers, and therefore it helps America.[196]

This speech was held in 2002 at the time when both the USA and the EC were expected to have already completed the implementation period of their Uruguay Round commitments. Instead of reducing domestic support programmes to farmers as expected, the Farm Bill increased such support by around 70 per cent. Furthermore, the US President put US agricultural products and US citizens at the same level of importance. The agricultural industry is not a second citizen in the USA, he said, and this industry must be protected as US citizens are protected. Domestically, markets will only be opened up if the farmers agreed to do so because a help to US farmers is a help to the USA. Of the farmers who receive subsidies in the USA, cotton growers are first among equals in the reaping of windfall financial gains from government transfers. Figure 1 below shows the scale of subsidies to US cotton farmers compared to other crops. The government's support to US's 25,000 cotton farmers is staggering and reflects the influence of corporate farm lobbies in key states. Every acre of cotton farmland in the US attracted in 2001/02 a subsidy of $230, the most subsidized crop in the US

---

196 The White House, Office of the Press Secretary, 13 May 2002, cited in Oxfam (2002b: 1)

agriculture. In comparison, the transfer to cereals was around five times less.

**Figure 1: Subsidy per Acre for Cotton and Related Crops in the USA, 2001/02, (US$)**

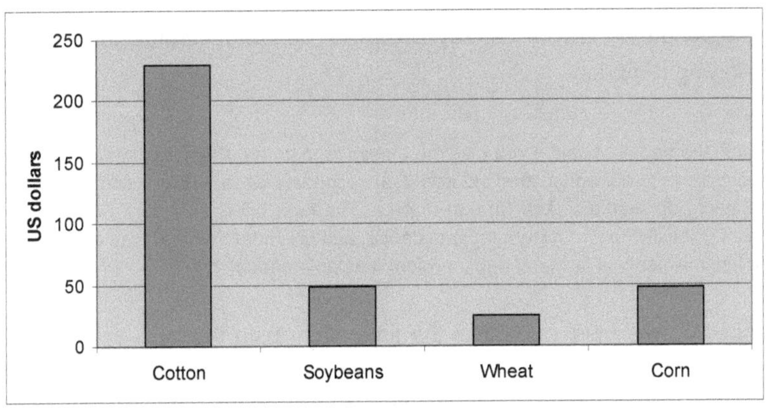


Source: *Agricultural Outlook, June/July 2002, cited by Oxfam (2002b: 33)*

The US Minnesota-based Institute for Agricultural and Trade Policy (IATP) states the USA is one of the world's largest sources of dumped agricultural commodities on world markets. In 2003, cotton was exported at an average price of 47 per cent below the cost of production.[197] The IATP study concludes that the levels of dumping were very consistent with the trend since the inception of WTO in 1995.[198] This revelation is a swipe at the global trade negotiations. It means that all efforts to liberalize agricultural trade do not bring any substantial changes in the USA agricultural domestic policy. In 2001/02, the value of outlays in the form of subsidies to cotton farmers by the US Department of Agriculture's Commodity Credit Corporation (CCC) was $3.9 billion. In other words, cotton was being produced at a net cost to

---

197 Sharma (2005)

198 Ibid.

other sectors of the US economy. Figure 2 shows the US cotton subsidies by category in the marketing year 2001 to 2002.

**Figure 2: US Cotton Subsidies by Category in 2001/02 ($m)**

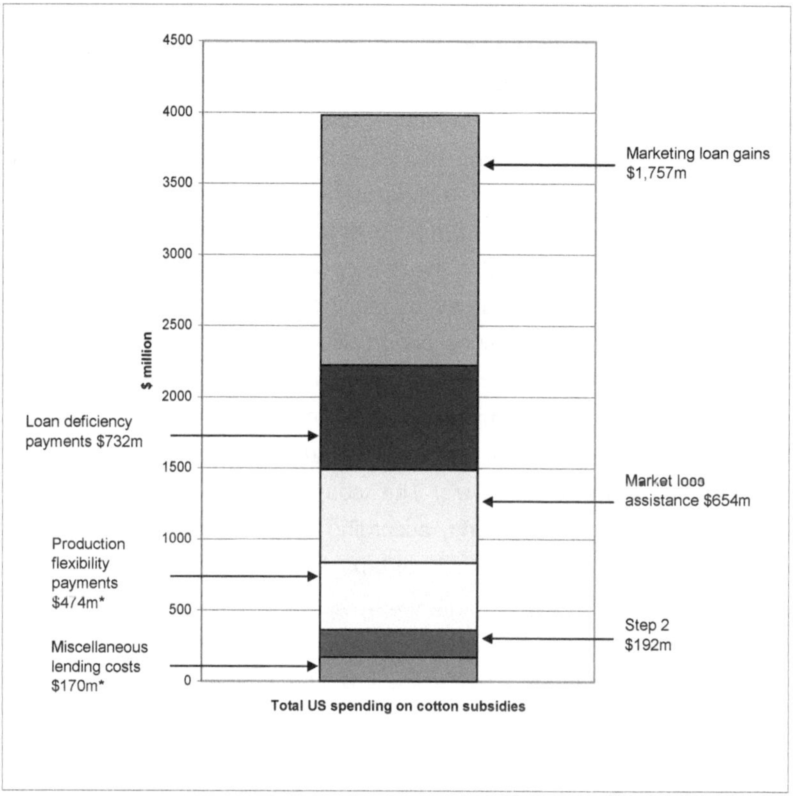

* Classified by the USDA as ‚green box' payments. All other payments are classified as 'amber box'.

Source: *US Department of Agriculture, cited by Oxfam (2002b: 14)*

As already laid down in the introductory part of this study, subsidies are identified in the World Trade Organization by boxes which are given the colour of traffic lights: 'green' is permitted, 'amber' means slow down and 'blue' are subsidies that require farmers to limit productions. These definitions have important bearing on trade negotiations among member of the world trading system. The main forms of US cotton subsidies are summarized in Figure 2.

Under the 2002 farm Bill, most cotton farmers benefit from direct payments based on the value of production and yields during a previous year of production period. Cotton farmers receive a direct payment of 6.66 cents per pound of cotton.[199] As the Agriculture Agreement recommends a 'decoupling' of payments to producers, that is, subsidies should not be paid to farmers based on their production capacities, the US government considers its payments to be decoupled from production and therefore eligible for the 'green box'. However, until 2002, the reference year for calculating payment levels was 1986-1988, as agreed during the Uruguay Round. Under the Farm Act of 2002, the reference period was updated to 1998-2001. This technical change matters because acreage under cotton and yields were higher in the latter period, which then raise the entitlement to subsidies.[200] This change means that subsidies were 'recoupled' to production by linking payments to recent output levels. The 'coupling' of production capacities with payments is trade-distorting, according to WTO rules. The US direct payments therefore fall into the 'amber box.'

Emergency market loss payments were replaced by counter-cyclical payments under the 2002 Farm Act. This subsidy is designed to increase payments to US cotton farmers during periods of low world prices. It thus enhances production at the time it should decline. Since such payments are based on the market price falling at a certain level, they fall into the 'amber box.'

---

[199] Rivoli (2005: 49)

[200] Oxfam (2002b: 15)

Loan deficiency payments and marketing loan gains are triggered when world prices fall below $0.52 per pound.[201] Such payments are linked to the volume of farm production and therefore also fall into the 'amber box.'

The step 2 subsidies aim to keep US export prices in line with low-cost competitors. They are provided both to exporters of US cotton and to domestic mills that use US cotton with an aim to eliminate any disparity between US internal prices and the international price. The transfer ranged in the 2001/02 marketing year from 0 to 7 cents per pound, what represented up to 18 per cent of the world price.[202]

Other lending costs include the Export Credit Guarantee Programme (ECGP) which borrows money to importers of US products at US interest rates, and banks lending to those importers, have the loans guaranteed by the US government. This gives US exporters an enormous advantage over rival exporters with shortage of hard currency or high interest rates. Another such programme is the US Crop Revenue and Insurance Programme that covers over 90 per cent of cotton acreage and protects farmers against crop loss caused by bad weather condition or other natural catastrophes. In total, the 2002 Farm Bill brought the US cotton farmer's income up to a minimum of 72.24 cents per pound, compared to average world price of cotton in mid-2004 of 38 cents per pound.[203]

From all these subsidies, the Step 2 payments and the Export Credit Guarantee are among the most damaging forms of subsidies, despite their relatively small size in overall terms. Step 2 payments are export subsidies that give US exporters a clear advantage over foreign competitors; the subsidy roughly offsets the difference between world market prices and US prices and therefore guarantees that US cotton is priced competitively in world markets. Export Credit Guarantee encourages foreign importers to buy products from the US market because they are granted loans at lower

---

201 Ibid. (p. 15)
202 Ibid. (p.15)
203 Rivoli (2005: 49)

rates. In case of insolvency, the US government is ready to step in and guaranty the liquidity to the banks. Only the US Crop Revenue and Insurance Programme could fall into the 'green box', because they are implemented using non-commodity specific intervention. They are permissible as long as they do not exceed the de minimis level of five per cent of the total value of production, as stated in the Agriculture Agreement.

However, not all US cotton farmers receive these payments. Farm subsidies are designed to reward and encourage large-scale, corporate production. The largest 10 per cent of cotton farms receive three quarters of total payments. In 2001, ten farms out of this 10 per cent received subsidies equivalent to $17million. Table 4 lists their ranks, names, the states where they are located as well as the amount of subsidies they received in 2001.

**Table 4: Top 10 Recipients of Cotton Subsidies in 2001**

| Rank | Name | State | Cotton subsidy for 2001, US $ | Total Farm subsidy for 2001, US $ |
|---|---|---|---|---|
| 1 | Tyler Farms | Arkansas | 5,993,748 | 8,089,543 |
| 2 | Dixie Farms | Mississippi | 1,694,392 | 2,282,054 |
| 3 | Ritchey Bayou Farm | Mississippi | 1,398,726 | 1,612,708 |
| 4 | Colorado River Indian Tribes Farm | Arizona | 1,146,266 | 1,389,312 |
| 5 | Bruton Farms Partnership | Mississippi | 1,144,571 | 1,532,998 |
| 6 | John M Mobley & Sons | Georgia | 1,142,589 | 1,207,711 |
| 7 | Martin Farm | Alabama | 1,062,742 | 1,146,315 |
| 8 | Benton Farms | Alabama | 1,011,266 | 1,278,012 |
| 9 | Due West | Mississippi | 1,009,631 | 1,205,916 |
| 10 | GPA Management Group | Arizona | 964,862 | 967,379 |
| | | **Total** | **16,568,793** | **20,711,948** |

Source: *Environmental Working Group Farm Subsidies Database, cited by Oxfam (2002b: 24)*

The US cotton farm belt extends across a large area from southern California in the West, through Texas and Arizona, to Mississippi, Alabama, and the Carolinas in the East. It covers approximately 14 million acres of land. The farm size ranges from 500 acres in the Carolinas and Mississippi to 2000 acres in the arid regions of the Texas Plains. The largest farm of the US is located in Central California with some 200,000 acres.[204] The political lobby for cotton is reported to be one of the strongest in US agriculture. Led by the National Cotton Council of America, the cotton barons foster an image of a sector dominated by farmers working in a harsh environment.[205] The corporate interests of the ten biggest cotton firms and the political lobby of the National Cotton Council of America undoubtedly make bargaining to liberalize agricultural trade difficult at the domestic level. Apart from Tyler and Dixie Farms, the total farm subsidy of the other top eight recipients is almost devoted to the cotton sector. This explains the economic dependence of these states on cotton, as well as magnifies the lobbying strength of their farmers.

Table 4 has shown that big farms are the beneficiary of US farm subsidies. According to USDA figures, the richest 10 per cent of American farmers receive two-thirds of total payments to agriculture. Those payments are concentrated among cotton producers, where the top 10 per cent receive 73 per cent of total payments.[206] Over the long term, these subsidies have enabled the US to expand its share of world cotton production from around 16 per cent at the start of the 1990s to over 20 per cent at the end of the decade.[207] A joint research conducted by the UN's Food and Agriculture Organization and the International Cotton Advisory Committee (ICAC) found that the withdrawal of subsidies would result in a decline in US production of 1.4 million tons, which is equivalent to 10 per cent. This overall effect

---

204 Oxfam (2002b: 22f)

205 Ibid. (p. 23)

206 Ibid. (p. 23)

207 Ibid. (p. 11)

would increase world prices by 11 cents per pound, or by almost 26 per cent.[208] From the perspective of conventional trade theory, the expansion of US cotton output is counter-intuitive. Market principles would dictate that, in an open market, prices would follow the costs of the more efficient producers. Less efficient, high cost producers will reduce production. In the world cotton production however, this principle is reversed. As far as the US agricultural trade policy is concerned, strategic trade policy is the cornerstone of this policy. Hence, the new view of trade theory is prevalent in the USA. But why does the US government transfer windfall subsidies only to cotton farmers and not to all farmers?

The theory of Anderson and Hayami can help answer this question. These authors predict that as comparative advantage shifts away from agriculture, governments will tend to protect the farming sector. Within the farming industry itself, farmers will lobby more for the protection of import-competing crops and less for the protection of the export-competing ones. Applying this theory to the US cotton protection offers some important insights. Does the US protect its cotton industry because she is a high-cost producer of that crop? The answer to this question will be forthcoming in the following sections.

## 5. 2. The European Community: Sugar Regime Reform?

The sugar sector of the EC is considered to be "one of the most distorted markets in European agriculture".[209] The sector has remained unchanged for almost 40 years.[210] The EC grows mainly sugar beet, but cane sugar is also processed in England. Sugar cane is a perennial grass grown in tropical areas, usually with a five year cropping circle whereas beet sugar is a root crop, mainly produced as part of an arable cycle. The EC beet sugar

---

208 Ibid. (13)
209 Oxfam (2004a: 1)
210 IP/06/194

accounts for almost 13 per cent of global sugar production.[211] Sugar beet is grown on around 230,000 holdings in the EC, usually alongside other crops, such as cereals, in rotation systems. Holdings where sugar beet grows are almost four times the average holding size for agriculture, while incomes on sugar beet holdings double the level of average income. For example, margins on sugar beet in eastern England are twice as high as those on cereals such as wheat and barley.[212] Among EC producers, France is by far the biggest producer of sugar, accounting for around one half of the total, followed by Germany and the United Kingdom. Figure 3 illustrates the share of the different countries in sugar export.

**Figure 3: Major EC Sugar Exporters 2003 (m tonnes)**

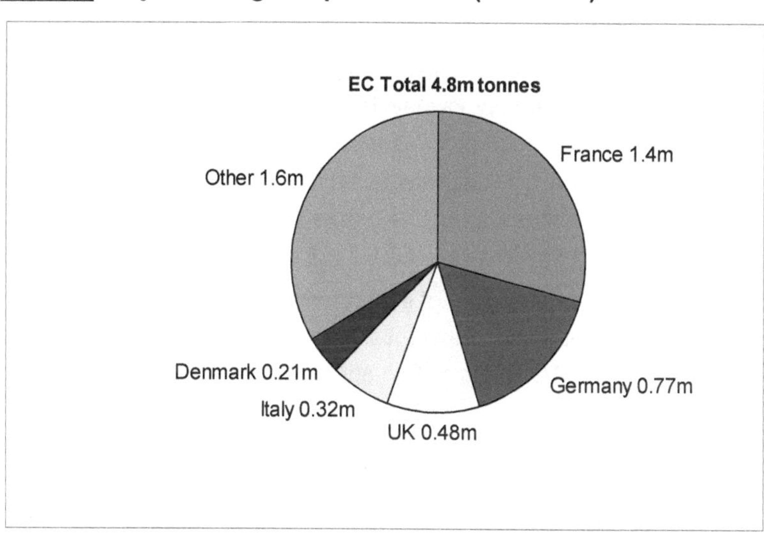


Source: *European Commission Data, cited by Oxfam (2004a: 15)*

211 Oxfam (2004a: 7)

212 Ibid. (p. 22)

With exports that oscillate around five million tonnes of sugar production a year, the EC is the second in overall share of the world market, behind Brazil. The CAP sugar regime rests on three legs, namely guaranteed prices, import protection, and export subsidies.

*Guaranteed prices* are applied to a quota that is determined yearly by the EC Commission. In recent years, quotas have been set at around 14 millions tonnes.[213] There is a structural surplus of around 1.5 million tonnes built into the quota system, making this an important source of the EC surplus that must be sold on world markets. Domestically, EC sugar processors were paid guaranteed prices of €632/ tonne for white sugar, compared with world market price o €157/ tonne in the marketing year 2004.[214] The domestic guaranteed price was approximately some three or four times above world prices.

*Import restrictions* are the counterpart to high guaranteed prices. Although world prices are locked at very low levels, it has been impossible for other exporters to enter the EC market for almost half a century.[215] On top of fixed tariff, the EC deploys a 'special safeguard' mechanism that increases as world prices fall. Current import duties create a tariff equivalent to around 324 per cent.[216]

*Export subsidies* are the opposite of import tariffs. The surplus built into the guaranteed price quota and preferential import from African, Caribbean, and Pacific countries (ACP) has to be kept out of the domestic market, so that guaranteed prices are not downsized. The preferred solution of the EC is to dump this surplus of production onto world markets. Export subsidies paid to processors and traders bridge the gap between domestic and world prices. The EC pays around €525/ tonne in export subsidies on quota sugar. That means, for every €1 in export earning generated by sugar sales, the EC spends around €3.30 in subsidies. Total refunds from the EC

---

213 Ibid. (p. 10)

214 Ibid. (p.10)

215 IP/06/194

216 Oxfam (2004a: 11)

budget amounted to €1.3 billion in 2002.[217] Figure 4 shows the CAP sugar regime in operation.

**Figure 4: The CAP Sugar Regime in Operation: Import Barriers and Export Subsidies (2004 prices)**

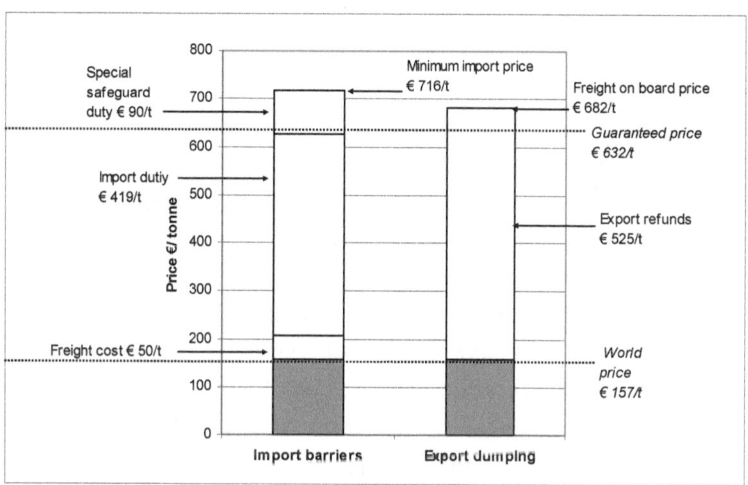


Source: *Based on Data from International Sugar Organization and European Commission, cited by Oxfam (2004a: 12)*

- The minimum import price on the EC market in the marketing year 2004 equalled to:

World price (€157/t) + freight cost (€50/t) + import duty (€419/) + special safeguard duty (€90/t) = €716/t.

- At the same period, the freight on board price equalled to:

World price (€157/t) + export refunds (€525/t) =€682/t.

---

[217] Ibid. (p. 11)

- The guaranteed price to EC processors and traders at the domestic market was €632/t.

- In order to export one tonne of sugar to the EC market, an additional duty of €559/ tonne was charged in 2004. At the same time, EC taxpayers and consumers paid an additional €525 for each tonne of sugar exported on foreign markets.

EC producers do not process only quota sugar. In addition to the 1.5 million tonnes of surplus in-quota sugar produced yearly by the EC, approximately 2.7 million tonnes of non-quota sugar is produced in a typical year.[218] Non-quota sugar can be produced without limit. However, under EC rules, non-quota sugar must be stored or sold without export subsidies on the international market.[219] Different parties to the World Trade Organization negotiations claim that subsidies on quota sugar 'spill over' into non-quota sugar, what creates a hidden cross-subsidy. In 2002, non-quota sugar represented one-quarter of total production, and around half of total exports.[220] Furthermore, due to an arrangement under the Sugar Protocol with the ACP countries, the EC imports yearly up to 1.6 million tonnes of sugar at guaranteed prices on a duty free basis. The EC sugar regime ensures that production that exceeds consumption levels is exported. Hence, EC taxpayers pay around €800 to €900 million to cover the cost of re-exporting the 1.6 million tonnes equivalent to ACP imports.[221] All this surplus of production is dumped on world markets. However, the CAP sugar regime does not benefit all EC beet growers and sugar processors, big processors reap the lion's share of government payments.

---

218 Ibid. (p.18)
219 Ibid. (p. 13)
220 Ibid. (p. 13)
221 Ibid. (p. 18)

According to Oxfam (2004a), the CAP sugar system is one of "corporate welfare through which powerful private interests capture the benefits of public policy."[222] Corporate control in the sugar sector is rooted in the quota system and processing firms are the gatekeepers of this system. They are allocated quotas by national governments who in turn license growers to produce fixed amounts of beet at guaranteed prices. Control over quotas is highly concentrated, mere six companies hold more than half of the total EC quota. The EC agricultural industry employs 52,000 people, and approximately 45,000 sugar beet growers.[223] Table 5 shows the names of these firms, the countries where they are located, their processing sector, and market control.

---

[222] Ibid. (p. 19)
[223] Ibid. (p. 44)

**Table 5: Top 6 Big Companies of the EC Sugar Processing**

| Country | Name | Processing sector | Market Control |
|---|---|---|---|
| **Britain** | Tate and Lyle | Cane Sugar | 90 % of British market |
| | British Sugar | Beet Sugar | |
| **France** | Beghin Say | Beet Sugar | One-third of French quota; One-half of Italian quota |
| **Germany** | Sudzucker | Beet Sugar | 40 % of German Market |
| **Denmark** | Danisco | Beet Sugar | Monopoly over quotas in Denmark, Sweden, Finland |
| **Spain** | Ebro Puerto | Beet Sugar | 80% of Spain quota |

*Summarized by G.N., read Oxfam (2004a: 20)*

Among those companies, the Sudzucker Group dominates the European market. It operates more than 56 sugar-processing factories across Europe. This includes four factories in the Raffinerie Tirlemontoise (RT) group in Belgium, which holds three-quarter of the national quota holder; five factories in France through the Saint Louis Sucre Group, the second largest quota holder in France; three factories in Agrana Group in Australia, the biggest national quota holder; and 14 factories in Poland.[224] The lobbying corporate at the centre of the sugar campaign is the Committee of European Sugar Manufacturers (or CEFS, the French acronym). Figure 5 is an estimation of export subsidies to selected companies.

224 Ibid. (p. 20)

**Figure 5: The Subsidy Harvesters: Estimated Export Subsidies to Selected Companies 2003 (€ m)**

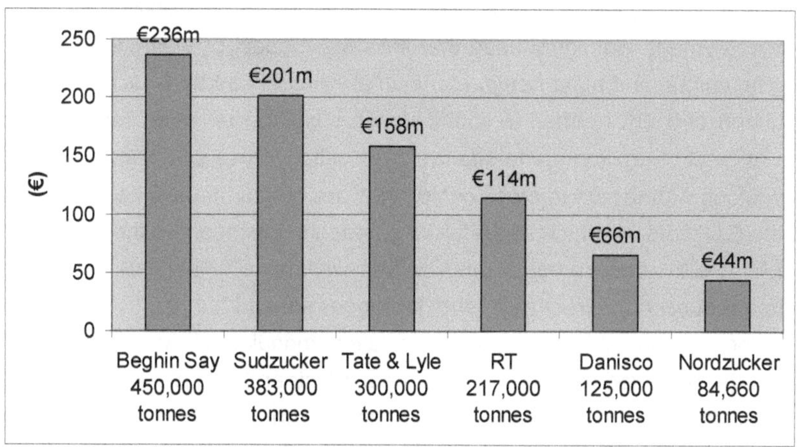


Source: *Oxfam Calculations (2004a: 25)*

As far as the sugar regime of the EC is concerned, strategic trade policy through government subsidies to EC sugar processing industry prevails. Like in the US agricultural policy, new views on trade theory are predominant here. The protection of corporate interests, imperfect competition through market monopoly, price guarantee, export subsidies, and the coupling of payments to production characterize the EC agricultural policy.

However, contrary to the US cotton regime, efforts to reform the CAP have been made in recent past by the EC Commission. On 26 June 2003, EC farm ministers adopted a fundamental reform of CAP. The innovation is that farmers are no longer paid just to produce food. "Today's CAP [2004] is demand-driven. It takes consumers' and taxpayers' concerns fully into account, while giving EU farmers the freedom to produce what the market wants. In future, the vast majority of aid to farmers will be paid independently of what or how much they produce."[225] The new CAP will be geared towards consumers' and taxpayers' needs. The link between subsidies and production has been severed, which makes EC farmers more competitive and market oriented, while providing them with income stability. A 'Single Farm Payment' was introduced that links the respect of environment, food safety, animal and plant health and animal welfare standards with good agricultural and environmental condition. This linkage between farming and the respect of environmental standards is called 'cross compliance'.[226] The provisions with regard to cross compliance are one of the new key elements in the CAP reform, which make future payments contingent to the respect of public health, environmental and animal welfare. The second innovation was a reduction in direct payments for bigger firms to finance the new rural development policy. This innovation is called 'modulation'. As payments will no longer be linked to production, farmers will steer their production towards the needs of the markets and the demands of the consumers. Decoupled payments mean that a major share of the EC support to agriculture is moved from the trade distorting 'amber box' to the minimal or non-trade distorting 'green box'. The single farm payment entered into force in 2005.[227] And on 1 July 2006, the EC sugar regime reform was enforced.[228]

A key element in the EC sugar reform was the establishment of a 'Restructuring Fund' financed by sugar producers to assist the restructuring process needed to make the industry competitive. The objective of this reform is to take out about 6 million tonnes of quota in order to ensure balance on the market after the transition period. The transition period lasts for four years (2006-2009).[229] For each year, 1.5 million tonnes are to be renounced. At the first year of application, about 1.5 million tonnes of quota were re-

225 European Communities (2004: 7)

226 European Commission (http://ec.europa.eu/agriculture/capreform/index_en.htm, retrieved on 14.02.2007)

227 Ibid.

228 IP/06/194

229 IP/06/1591

nounced. And this trend is expected to continue for the next production year, starting on 1 October 2007. In order to encourage producers to give up their quotas, "each tonne of quota renounced was compensated with 730 €/t from the restructuring fund. This is also the level 2007/08, but the restructuring aid then falls to 625 €/t in 2008/09 and 520 €/t in 2009/10, the fourth and final year."[230] This restructuring fund is a carrot to allow uncompetitive sugar producers to leave the industry. The fund is sourced by payments by sugar, isoglucose and inulin producers according to their production quota.[231] EC production is expected to fall by 6 and 7 million tonnes, what will allow the EC to open its market completely to imports from the world's poorest countries from 2009.[232] The key to the reform is a 36 per cent cut in the guaranteed minimum sugar price[233]. This cut will set the guaranteed price at around €227/tonne, i.e. less than one-half of world prices if they were stabilized at €157/ tonne. If this reform succeeds, by the year 2010, the EC could ensure balance on the domestic sugar market, whilst at the same time reduce, or end the dumping of its surplus sugar production on world markets. This reform intends to bring the regime in compliance with WTO rules with a view to appease the complaints of some G20 member states.

## 5.3. The G20: Impact of Agricultural Policy

As already discussed in chapter 3, the demands of the G20 in global trade talks are threefold: the group wants to access the US and EC domestic markets; it needs a new deal for cotton farmers in some West African countries; and finally it opposes the inclusion of new issues into the Doha agenda.

---

230 Ibid.
231 Ibid.
232 IP/06/194
233 Ibid.

The July Package met some of these demands: Of the four new issues that the EC wanted to include into the agenda, only 'trade facilitation' was maintained. A sub-committee on cotton was established that regularly meets and reports its findings to the Committee of Agriculture; and the USA and EC were reminded of their commitments to open up domestic markets to products originating from the G20 countries and vice-versa. Whereas the July Package solved the problem of new issues, the question of agricultural trade-distorting domestic subsidies remained inconclusive. This subsection tackles the impact of cotton and sugar on the farming sector of some member states of the G20.

Since the Cancún Ministerial Conference of 2003, cotton has been one the major items on the WTO negotiation agenda. In West Africa alone, "10 million people depend on cotton for their livelihoods. US cotton dumping, causing a sharp decline in world cotton prices, has impoverished all of these farmers."[234] Such decline in world cotton prices affects the farming sector of many members of the G20, as well. Therefore, Brazil brought a case at the WTO against US cotton subsidies.

In 2004, a dispute settlement panel adjudicated and found that US cotton subsidies are contrary to WTO rules. Table 6 summarizes the finding of the WTO panel in this respect.

---

234 Oxfam (2004b: 1)

**Table 6: Implications of the Ruling on US Subsidy Programmes on Cotton and Export Credits**

| US programmes challenged in the dispute | Total amount for 2002/2003 ($bn) | Classification notified by the USA to the WTO | Panel decision about box classification | Other panel recommendations(i) |
|---|---|---|---|---|
| Export credits (cotton and other commodities) (ii) | 1.6 | Not notified | Export subsidies | To be eliminated |
| Step 2 (cotton) | 0.4 | Amber box | Export subsidies | To be eliminated |
| Marketing loan payments (cotton) | 0.9 | Amber box | Amber box | To be eliminated |
| Countercyclical payments (cotton) | 1.3 | Amber box | Amber box | To be eliminated |
| Direct payments (cotton) | 0.6 | Green box | Amber box | Reclassification in amber box |

(i)Panel recommendations relative to rules on export subsidies and to the serious prejudice claim linked with the price-suppressing effect.
(ii) Export credits for cotton, soybeans, corn, oilseed, oil products, and rice.

Source: *Data from Brazil's Submission to the Panel and the US Notifications to the WTO, cited by Oxfam (2004b: 4)*

The WTO panel found that the USA used hidden subsidies to circumvent its WTO commitments. These subsidies were found contrary to WTO rules and were ordered to be eliminated. The panel findings can be summarized as follows: the US credits, worth of $1.6 billion in 2002, constitute export subsidies; the Step 2 programme constitutes an export subsidy rather than trade distorting domestic support; and finally, direct payments on cotton are not minimally trade-distorting. Therefore, they cannot be classified as green box payments; the panel classified them as trade distorting domestic support into the amber box. These findings shed light on the serious prejudice caused by the US domestic support to the G20 farming, and especially to some West African countries. The lost to the latter group of countries as a result of US subsidies has been incommensurable. The next table (7) is based on calculations of the International Cotton Advisory Committee (ICAC) to measure the extent of such loss.[235]

**Table 7: Foreign Exchange Losses as a Result of US Cotton Subsidies in Selected Countries in West Africa ($m)**

| Country | Actual cotton export earnings in 2001/02, in $m | Export earnings with the withdrawal of US subsidies, in $m* | Value lost as a result of US subsidies, in $m |
|---|---|---|---|
| **Benin** | 124 | 157 | 33 |
| **Burkina Faso** | 105 | 133 | 28 |
| **Cameroon** | 81 | 102 | 21 |
| **Central African Rep.** | 9 | 12 | 2 |
| **Chad** | 63 | 79 | 16 |
| **Ivory Coast** | 121 | 153 | 32 |
| **Mali** | 161 | 204 | 43 |
| **Togo** | 61 | 77 | 16 |
| **Total** | **725** | **917** | **191** |

*Using ICAC model result predicting an 11 cents/lb net increase in world cotton

Source: *International Cotton Advisory Committee, cited by Oxfam (2002b: 18)*

According to the World Bank, Burkina Faso, Mali, and Benin are among the lowest-cost producers of cotton.[236] Costs of production for one pound of cotton are three times higher in the USA than in Burkina Faso, for example.[237] Yet despite this comparative advantage, these West African countries have lost world market share to the US cotton growers. The ICAC considers that

---

[235] These West African countries are not members of the G20. However, they are included here in the analysis because their concerns were echoed by the G20 at the negotiating table of the WTO. Of the three demands brought by the G20, one of them focused on the cotton issue of these countries. In many instances, member states of the G77 and of the G90, which lack negotiating power, join sometimes with the G20 for matters related to their interests.

[236] Read Oxfam (2002b: 2)

[237] Ibid.

the USA is liable for the slump in world cotton prices. Its estimates indicate that the withdrawal of American cotton subsidies would raise cotton prices by 11 cents per pound, or by 26 per cent.[238] Such increase in cotton price could boost production in West Africa and among the G20 member states. The government of India puts the total cost of US subsidies at $1.3 billions, Argentina puts it at more than $1 billion, and the Brazilian government claims losses of $640 million for 2001/2002.[239]

Before global trade negotiations came to a halt in July 2006, the USTR Rob Portman announced the launch of the West Africa Cotton Improvement Programme (WACIP) to correct this state of affairs. The program aimed at the cotton sectors of Benin, Burkina Faso, Chad, Mali and Senegal. "The west Africa Cotton Improvement Program is one more way the United States is specially addressing the needs of cotton dependent countries in Africa,"[240] said Ambassador Portman. "When combined with [...] administration effort to end the Step 2 cotton program and a bold proposal on agriculture in the World Trade Organizations, the United States has taken real steps that can help West Africa, including its cotton farmers."[241] With the deadlock in agricultural negotiations, the probability that the US government fulfils its obligations under the WTO rules has become a rather problematic one.

Let me now turn to the EC sugar regime and its impact on the G20 farming sector. With around 5 million tonnes of sugar export a year, the EC is second to Brazil in overall share of the world market. The top seven sugar exporters account for around half of world exports.[242] Apart from the EC, no other country, than member states of the G20 is an efficient producer of raw sugar. Brazil is by far the biggest exporter of sugar on world markets. Fig-

---

238 Ibid.
239 Ibid. (p. 8)
240 USTR, Press Release (2005c)
241 Ibid.
242 Oxfam (2004a: 8)

ure 6 shows the world sugar exports of selected countries between 2001 and 2003.

**Figure 6: World Sugar Exports: Selected Countries (2001-2003 Average)**

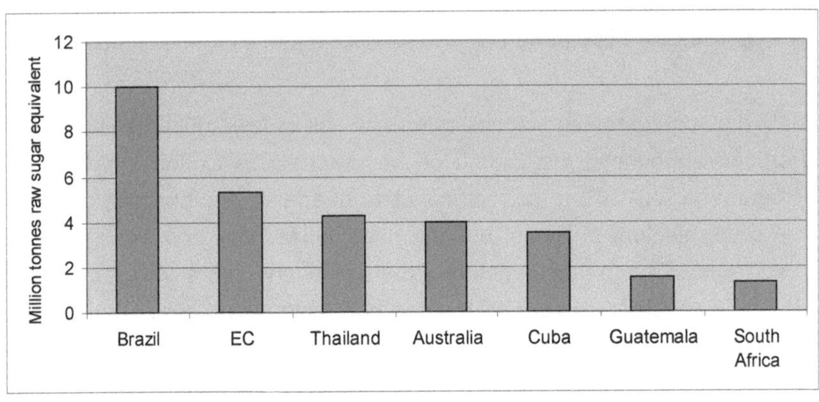


Source: *National Sugar Organization Data, cited by Oxfam (2004a: 8)*

Here again, Brazil, Thailand and Australia brought a charge against the EC sugar regime at the WTO.[243] Their complaint was based on the grounds that the EC 'cross-subsidizes' exports of non-quota sugar, indirectly subsidizes export of quota sugar, and directly subsidizes exports of a further amount equivalent to ACP imports.[244] The WTO panel ruling on this matter, found that the EC indeed dumps significant amounts of subsidized sugar, more than allowed by the WTO rules. The panel findings can be summarized in three main points.

First, the panel found that the export of 2.7 million tonnes of what the EC claimed to be *unsubsidized sugar* (the so-called non-quota or 'C' sugar),

---

243 Oxfam (2004c)

244 Oxfam (2004a: 16)

are effectively *cross-subsidized* by EC support provided for the production of quota sugar. These cross-subsidies allow the EC to sell non-quota 'C' sugar at prices below the cost of production because the prices for quota sugar are sufficient to cover also the fixed cost of production of non-quota sugar. Second, the panel also ruled that the EC contravenes its WTO commitments by subsidizing the re-export of an amount equivalent to imports of sugar from the ACP countries and India. The panel, however, did not interfere with the right of the EC to import sugar from the ACP and India on preferential terms. Finally, the panel recommended that the EC reforms its sugar regime in a way that will protect preferential access for ACP countries and India.[245]

One of the most widely used economic models designed to assess the scale of the costs to the G20 exporting countries predicts that the removal of distortions associated with the CAP sugar regime would increase international prices by 20 to 23 per cent, with sugar cane growers expanding their market share.[246] Taking the 2002 exports as a basis for calculation, and assuming that the CAP lowers the unit value of those exports by 23 per cent, Oxfam estimates the immediate losses associated with CAP-sponsored sugar dumping at $494 million for Brazil, $151 million for Thailand, $64 million for India, and $60 million for South Africa.[247]

To sum up, this chapter offers four main findings:

(i) As far as agricultural trade policy is concerned, the USA and the EC share the new view of trade theory, for which strategic trade policies and imperfect competition are the cornerstone.

In the USA, interests of 'cotton barons' are represented by the National Cotton Council of America where ten big cotton farms absorb more than half of government transfers. In the EC, the interests of sugar farmers are coordi-

245 Oxfam (2004c: 2)

246 Oxfam (2004a: 28)

247 Ibid. (p. 28-31)

nated by the Committee of European Sugar Manufacturers. Here, too, six big processors control more than half of the EC sugar quota.

(ii) Whereas these strategic trade policies allow US and EC farmers to secure big shares on world markets, they impact negatively on the farming sector of the G20.

(iii) The protection of farmers' and corporate interests make it difficult for the US and EC governments to ratify agreements at the domestic level.
Domestic constituencies show less willingness to ratify agreements that might put their interests at risk. Their motto is that 'no agreement is better than a bad agreement'.

(iv) The game for the provision of the public good – agricultural trade liberalization – is to be understood as a graduated, rather than a simple two-by-two matrix prisoner's dilemma.
As discussed throughout this chapter, other policy alternatives are there for the USA and the EC than just the Pareto optimal payoff (**3, 3**), or the Nash equilibrium (**2, 2**). In other words, the USA and the EC do not just have two choices, either to liberalize or to protect. Their respective cotton and sugar regimes exhibit other possible cooperative trends.

To illustrate this last point, the US ambassador Rob Portman promised to some West African countries that his government will remove the Step 2 subsidies in the near future. Other efforts are made by the US government to classify its direct payments to cotton farmers into the green box, although, the WTO panel proved the contrary. In the end, there is a mixture of liberalization and protection trends in respect to the US cotton regime. This mixture makes it difficult to classify the US policy choice, as typically protective or typically liberal. In short, the USA played strategies that were predominantly located outside the **JKL** cells, at the eastern side of Table 3.

Like the USA, the EC sugar regime offers intermediate policy alternatives. However, contrary to the US cotton regime, policy choices of the EC have been relocated within the **JKL** upper left hand, Pareto optimal outcome, of Table 3. This difference in policy choices can be explained as follows: Since 2003, the EC has undertaken a reform of the CAP and on 1 July 2006, the sugar regime reform came into force. Despite the stalemate in agricultural trade negotiations, the EC is committed to balance its domestic market of sugar by the year 2009/10. The first year of implementation period was successful, as sugar growers indeed gave up 1.5 million tonnes of sugar as expected. The EC is committed to remove its trade-distorting domestic support to sugar beet growers and processors from the amber box to the green box. The US Farm Bill of 2002, on the contrary, increased subsidies to US farmers by 70 per cent for a period of ten years (until 2012). Therefore, the EC is considered to be more cooperative in the provision of the public good than the USA. As far as cotton and sugar regimes are concerned, the level of cooperation of the US government can be rated between policy choices (**.5** and **.75**), while the EC level of cooperation may be located between strategies (**.25** and **.5**) of Table 3.[248] From what has been said, it becomes evident that policy choices of the different parties lead to Pareto suboptimal outcomes. Was there a way to yield a Pareto efficient outcome?

[248] This estimation is based on the US cotton and EC sugar regimes during the Doha trade talks (2001-2006).

# 6. Overcoming the Stalemate?

This chapter explores the different alternatives that can help overcome the deadlock in agricultural trade liberalization. As noted earlier, the stalemate in global trade talks is directly related to involuntary defection. Faced with the choice to ratify an international agreement or not to ratify it, domestic interest groups usually ask two interrelated questions: 'What could we gain if we ratify such agreement and/or what could we loose if we fail to do so?' In cases where the gains of 'no-ratification' are negligible and the costs for 'ratification' high, domestic constituencies intend to vote down the international agreement. Henceforth, the very concern at Level II is the size of win-sets.

## 6.1. Taking Win-Sets Seriously

According to Putnam, larger win-sets make Level I agreements more likely, because such win-sets fall within the Level II preferences of each of the parties to the accord. Thus, ratification of Level I agreements is only possible if those win-sets overlap or ensure joint gains. By the same token, perceived larger win-sets of one negotiator at Level I are a bargaining disadvantage, while a small domestic win-set is a bargaining advantage. Conversely, the smaller the win-sets are, the greater the risk of involuntary defection. To put the issue in a nutshell, there are different strategies that lead to a successful ratification of international agreements: First, larger win-sets with overlapping interests among negotiators lead to successful ratification, all other things being equal; second, a perceived larger win-set for one negotiator ushers in a 'no-ratification' by other domestic constituencies; third, a small domestic win-set is a bargaining advantage; and finally it is difficult to negotiate with democracies for whom ratification of international agreements requires a two-third majority.

One may therefore ask following questions: Did the win-sets between the USA, the EC and the G20 overlap during agricultural trade negotiations? Did one country or a group thereof secure larger win-sets at the expense of others? Which country enjoyed a bargaining advantage? And finally, were democracies involved in negotiations, for which a two-third majority system requires ratification of international agreements? These four questions are answered below in Table 8.[249]

**Table 8: Results of Bargaining Strategies between the USA, the EC and the G20**

| | Overlapping interests | Securing larger win-sets | Bargaining advantage | Two-third majority |
|---|---|---|---|---|
| **United States** | USA/ EC | No | Yes | Yes |
| **European Community**[250] | EC/ USA | Yes | No | Yes, Unanimity required |
| **G20** | G20 vs. USA/ EC | Yes | No | Mix |

This table yields following results for the three groups of countries:

(i) Starting with the USA, her interests overlapped with those of the EC. Both parties pledged for lower cuts in agricultural subsidies and needed domestic support to their farmers; both were more or less willing to open up their markets for agricultural goods originating from member states with which they do not have preferential agreements. Furthermore, of the four new issues introduced by the EC in the Doha Agenda, the US government

249 Assessment criteria are grounded on Chapter 3 of this study that deals wit the 'Dynamic of Negotiations'.

250 Only declarations of the EC trade commissioner are accounted for here. If the Counsel of EC agricultural ministers unanimously agree at the community level to reform the CAP, their respective national governments will implement such agreement, irrespective of their internal legal provisions.

supported two. The USA did not want to secure larger win-sets.[251] This may be partly explained by the fact that, as the main exporter of agricultural goods on world markets, the USA already enjoys such large win-sets. This position allowed the US government to enjoy a bargaining advantage in the negotiations. And finally, the US constitution requires a two-third majority voting for ratification of international agreements. Does this requirement also hold for the EC?

(ii) Interests of the EC and the USA intersected, for the same reasons, as noted above. However, this intersection of interests did not hold too long, as the EC, contrary to the USA, wanted to secure larger win-sets. In other words, the EC was against larger cuts in export subsidies and domestic support; it wanted to include four 'new issues' into the negotiating agenda, so that EC firms can efficiently compete on world markets. To deduce from this behaviour means that the EC lacked a bargaining advantage and was 'pushed around' by the other Level I negotiators. And finally, the EC law requires unanimity to reform the CAP. What about the G20?

(iii) Interests of the G20 conflicted with those of the USA and the EC. Like the EC however, the G20 wanted to secure larger win-sets: the group was against the introduction of new issues that could lead to the dismantlement of its protectionist measures. In addition, the G20 demanded simultaneously a radical reform of the CAP, large cuts in the three pillars of agricultural trade liberalization, and compensations from the USA and the EC for losses incurred to the G20 farming sector. The group, however, was unwilling to substantially reduce its tariff barriers for the US and EC manufacturers and service providers. Lastly, the G20 constitutions are mixed.

---

251 The failure to ratify the Level I agreements by the US Congress was, according to the US government statements, due to the lack of reciprocity that US farmers deplored. Reciprocity here should not be equated with the need to secure large win-sets. Reciprocity is a rule-based condition for trade liberalization; read Article XXXVIII bis of GATT.

In sum, one can say that Putnam's second proposition about the size of the win-set that depends on the Level II political institutions was a determinant factor for the failure to ratify agreements at Level II. In other words, the demands of domestic interest groups together with domestic institutions led to the breakdown of negotiations. A 'no-ratification' vote at Level II does not pit the Level I agreement against other alternatives, it rather opens up negotiations at Level I anew. For international organizations such as the WTO that requires unanimity, any unilateral defection can block further negotiations. Is there a way out of this blockade? Can internal side-payments and/or synergic linkage remedy this situation?

### *6.1.1. Internal Side-Payments and Synergic Linkages*

According to Mayer (1992), "internal side-payments should be most useful in cases such as agricultural trade."[252] Internal side-payments are agreements that link side-issues on which to compensate potential losers for greater liberalization of trade. Such payments could be designed in two different ways: across different sectors of the national economy (manufacturers that compensate farmers or vice-versa); or they could be employed within the same sector (farmers that compensate farmers or manufacturers that compensate manufacturers).

If the factors of production are specific to domestic industries, the owners of factors employed in the export-competing industry could compensate the owners of factors of production employed in the import-competing one. In this way, the import-competing industry could be willing to support the export-competing one for free trade, as the gains from trade are internally redistributed without reducing the national welfare. If the factors of production are mobile across industries, the owners of the abundant factor could redistribute their gains internally to the owners of the scarce factors who are the net losers of free trade. In this way, the net losers could support the winners of trade liberalization in their campaign for free trade. Within the same sector, the owners of the export-competing crops could redistribute their gains to the owners of the import-competing crops. In all of these cases, the liberalization of trade will ensure joint gains to both the winners and losers of free trade without affecting negatively the national welfare.

The usage of internal side-payments is not new in the history of trade liberalization. In 1988, the success of the USA to negotiate with Japan for a more open market for US beef and citrus was only made possible largely by the willingness of the Japanese government to make a side-payment to Japanese agricultural interests in "the form of increased subsidies to beef producers."[253] Similarly, during the Tokyo Round of GATT, the USA and the EC reached bilateral accords on several commodities, including cheese, lamb, wool, barley, tobacco, rice, and prunes. Such agreements were made possible because of "the ability of the EC commission to link side-issues on which to compensate potential losers from greater liberalization."[254] The importance of internal side-payments can also be illustrated in the current agricultural trade negotiations.

Since 1 July 2006, the EC commission agreed to use internal side-payments for the reduction of its domestic production of sugar. The farmers who are willing to give up their quota for sugar production receive a payment equivalent to the value of production given up.[255]

However, designing side-payments is not an easy task: "Arranging side-payments is not necessarily a simple task. If it were easy, presumably they

---

252 Mayer (1992: 810)

253 Ibid. (p. 810)

254 Ibid. (p. 810)

255 At the time of writing, the EC farmers indeed gave up 1.5 million tonnes of sugar for the first marketing year 2006/2007 as expected. If this trend continues, by the year 2009/10, the EC would have already succeeded in balancing its domestic market of sugar.

would be made as a matter of course."[256] Nevertheless, the difficulty in such arrangement does not invalidate its policy implication to gain support from net losers of trade liberalization at Level II. Another policy option besides internal-side payments is the entanglement of domestic and international politics in such a way that the success obtained at the one level ushers in a success at the other level. Putnam calls this type of linkage synergic linkage.

The strategy of synergic linkage does not work by changing the preferences of any domestic constituents, but rather by creating a policy option.[257] Synergic linkages concern the type of relationship between issue-linkage at Level I that alters the feasible outcomes at Level II. In other words, the interests of domestic groups are taken into account for any agreement made at Level I. Such entanglements were made possible in the Agriculture Agreement and the July Package. Some states demanded a 'special status' for a number of their agricultural products and got it. The July Package also offered a leeway to the parties to elect some goods as 'Sensitive'. In addition, the G20 was allowed to elect some products as 'Special Products' that would be exempted from liberalization after negotiation with the other members. Policy options are indeed found in both agreements. However, there is still a need for more policy options granted to Level II. Agreements of Level I that aim at completely changing the preferences of domestic interest groups without creating policy options have less chance to be ratified at Level II. It may be the case that the creation of policy options is the key to success, although the attempt to meet the demands of each party could lead to the breakdown of the multilateral system as a whole, as each party will intend to veto for its own preferences.

---

256 Mayer (1992: 816)
257 Putnam (1988: 447)

# 7. Conclusion

The aim of this study has been to examine, 'why is agricultural trade liberalization at a stalemate?' In order to carry this out, multilateral negotiations between the United States, the European Community and the G20 during the Doha Round were analysed.

The first chapter dealt with the three pillars of agricultural trade liberalization, (market access, domestic support, export subsidies); it worked out the relevance of the research question; analysed three general criteria of research design (plenitude, boundedness, representativeness) and finally introduced the organizational part.

Chapter two was devoted to both the liberal theory of international relations and to the trade theories. With the 'bottom up' view of the liberal theory of IR, 'states' representatives at Level I are seen as 'transmission belts' of preferences and interests of domestic groups and coalitions. The subsection of this chapter depicted three variants of trade theories. One variant was the classical theories of Adam Smith and David Ricardo, another variant the neo-classical theories of Eli Heckscher and Bertil Ohlin, Wolfgang Stolper and Paul Samuelson, K. Anderson and Y. Hayami; and lastly the new trade theories of Michael Spence, Avinash Dixit, or Joseph Stiglitz.

Classical trade theories assume that differences in technology and tastes are the causes of trade. The Neo-classical theories emphasize two facts. First, the conflict of interests between the owners of both the abundant factors and scarce factors of production is the driving force that leads to trade (Heckscher-Ohlin model), or that factor price change is the consequence of trade (Stolper-Samuelson model). Second, policy protection shifts from industry to agriculture, as comparative advantage shifts away from agriculture

(Anderson-Hayami model).[258] Whilst, proponents of the new trade theory share the view that trade is driven by increasing returns to scale and imperfect competition.

The common denominator for all these theories is that the conflict of interests at the domestic level determines the support for, or the opposition to, free trade.

The third chapter was devoted to the dynamics of negotiations. This chapter started by defining the concept 'multilateralism' in general terms. Quantitatively, multilateralism refers to the cooperation between three or more states, and qualitatively, it refers to the rules of conduct among the parties, irrespective of their self-interests. In specific terms, multilateralism was defined according to the Most-Favoured-Nation (MFN) clause of the GATT (Article I). Thereafter, it followed the logic of two-level games, propounded by Robert Putnam. Negotiations at the different levels (I, II, III) helped to work out the strategies used by the different parties engaged in negotiations. Starting with the USA, her agricultural policy prior to 2001 was first contextualized, and then the games played at the different levels, analysed. The same procedure was used for the other two parties. However, contrary to the two-level game played by the USA; the EC played a three-level game in global trade negotiations. Level I represented international negotiations, Level II negotiations at the community level and Level III, negotiations at the national levels. Likewise, for member states of the G20, negotiations also took place at two levels.

Chapter four focused on the outcome of negotiations. It started with the July Package, a post-Cancún decision of the General Council of the WTO that aimed to re-launch the Doha Round negotiations, and continued with the discussion related to the implementation of the Agriculture Agreements. Ag-

---

[258] Although the theory of Anderson and Hayami was recently developed [after the 1970s], it nevertheless falls under the category of neo-classical theories. Anderson and Hayami still share the opinion that comparative advantage is the driving force that leads to international trade.

ricultural trade liberalization was depicted as a public good, i.e. a good which is 'non-excludable' and 'jointly supplied'. Since more than 150 states are members of the WTO, the incentives to renege on their commitments, while at the same time taking advantages of privileges granted by others, are very high. The issues raised here were that of a 'collective action problem' and of a 'prisoner's dilemma game'. Each party engaged in negotiations knew that it could gain from free trade, if the others liberalized, whilst using protectionist measures in return. Therefore, all the parties ended up playing the protectionist strategy, that lead to a Pareto sub optimal outcome, and hence to the stalemate in negotiations.

Having regarded agricultural trade liberalization as a collective action problem and the game played as a graduated prisoner's dilemma, chapter five discussed the explanatory power of the theories. It started with the reform of the US cotton and EC sugar regimes, and concluded with the impact of agricultural policy on the G20.

Instead of reducing its domestic support programmes as required by the Agriculture Agreements, the US Farm Bill of 2002 increased payments to farmers by 70 per cent (until 2012). According to WTO rules, the US cotton regime fell under the category 'trade-distorting' policy. It was possible to show that the USA shared the view of new trade theories.

The EC sugar regime also fell under the rubric 'trade-distorting' policy, as defined by WTO rules. Like the USA, the EC shared also the view of new trade theories. However, the EC launched a reform programme of its common agricultural policy (2003) that led to the sugar reform of 1 July 2006. With this sugar reform, the EC moved its sugar regime from the amber to the green box.

After comparing the levels of cooperation of the USA and the EC for the provision of the public good, the USA strategies were rated at (.5 and .75) and those of the EC at (.25 and .50). These policy choices meant that the EC was more cooperative than the USA for the provision of the public good, in this case – agricultural trade liberalization.

The last section of this chapter dealt with the impact of agricultural trade policy of the USA and the EC on member states of the G20. The impact of such policies was seen as detrimental for the economic development of these countries. It was pointed out that strategic trade policies of the USA and the EC deter the G20's farmers from entry into world markets.

Chapter six dealt with the question of whether the stalemate can be overcome. In this respect, four criteria that influence the outcome of negotiations were sorted out. First, it was found out that negotiations are likely to succeed when the interests of negotiating partners overlap. Second, parties that secure large win-sets are 'pushed around' by the other international partners in negotiations. Third, parties that secure smaller win-sets enjoy a bargaining advantage, as their proposals can be accepted by the domestic constituents of the other negotiators. And lastly, countries, whose political institutions demand a two-third majority voting or unanimity for ratification of international agreements, register a high level of involuntary defection. Hence, win-sets were seen as the cornerstone for ratification of Level I agreements at Level II and III. If win-sets were seriously taken, it would have been possible to reach a breakthrough in agricultural trade negotiations. Two concepts, internal side-payments and synergic linkages, were introduced in this respect.

Internal side-payments were used in negotiations between the USA and Japan (1988) for a more open market for US beef and citrus. Regarding this, the Japanese government made a side payment to Japanese beef producers to gain their support. Also during the Tokyo Round, the USA and the EC reached bilateral agreements on several commodities, which were influenced by the ability of the European Commission to compensate potential losers for greater liberalization. Since 1 July 2006, the EC commission once again used side-payments to reduce the domestic production of sugar. Synergic linkages are the counterpart to internal side-payments

Synergic linkages work by creating policy options for domestic constituencies. The Agriculture Agreement and the July Package offered such policy options. Countries that demanded a 'Special Status' for some of their main protected products, were able to achieve their demands. The July Package allowed each party to select some products, otherwise called 'sensitive', to be exempted from liberalization. Furthermore, all member states of the G20 were additionally allowed to negotiate with the other parties on a number of 'Special Products' that could also be exempted from a radical liberalization.

In summary, this study has offered five main findings:

(i) Countries, whose negotiators are engaged in multilateral negotiations, have to play games at the different board settings of the table, in order to reform their agricultural trade policies. However, even high skilled negotiators face difficulties to broker a deal in trans-border agricultural trade because "self-sufficiency in basic foodstuffs has been a priority of governments throughout history, and state authorities rarely feel comfortable unless they have made efforts to reduce their reliance on foreign supplies to feed their people."[259] In the past, governments easily regulated the domestic markets of agricultural trade, while opening the manufactured goods to free trade. These protectionist policies have been challenged during the Doha trade talks, and their reform require negotiations at the different levels of the game.

(ii) Agricultural trade liberalization is a prisoner's dilemma game. However, this game is not a simple two-by-two matrix prisoner's dilemma. It is a graduated game, because between the Pareto efficient outcome (3, 3) and the Nash Equilibrium (2, 2), there are intermediate policy alternatives available to the different parties. In the process of agricultural trade liberalization, countries neither totally cooperate with each other, nor totally defect from each other. Their policy choices are a mixture of, more or less, cooperation and defection.

---

[259] Mahler (1991: 31)

(iii) The stalemate in agricultural trade liberalization is not linked to the inability of member states of the multilateral trading system to make agreements at Level I. The problem stems from their implementation at Levels II and III, as illustrated by the Agriculture Agreement (1995), and the July Package (2004). Both agreements face difficulties for their implementation at the domestic level.

(iv) The protection of corporate interests of big farms that reap windfall government payments explain why ratification of Level I agreements fail at the domestic level. In the USA, 10 big farms represented by the National Cotton Council of America block any ratification of agreements that hurt their interests. In the EC, six big companies that operate in the sugar processing sector, dominate the European sugar market. The interests of those sugar processors are represented by the Committee of European Sugar Manufacturers.

(v) There are possible ways to overcome the stalemate in agricultural trade liberalization. If win-sets are taken seriously by all the parties to negotiations, a breakthrough is possible. The setting up of internal compensation mechanisms, where the winners of free trade can reward the net losers of agricultural trade liberalization is a way, in which the stalemate can be overcome. Another way is the entanglement of domestic and international interests in such a manner that both can overlap. If the interests of domestic interest groups are taken into account, when making agreements at Level I, policy options can be created that make it easy for domestic constituency to identify with Level I agreements.

This study was a modest attempt to answer a rather difficult question: why is agricultural trade liberalization at a stalemate? While many researchers adopt a descriptive approach to point out the messiness in agriculture trade, my attempt has been to explore the issue and offer some solutions to overcome the stalemate. As the liberalization of agricultural trade is an ongoing process, I wish that multilateralism becomes possible in trans-border agricultural trade like this is the case in other sectors.

## Bibliography


Agreement on Agriculture 1994, (LT/UR/A-A1/2), 15 April.

Ahern Bertie 2005: "We must stand by the Common Agricultural Policy", *Financial Times*, 26 September.

Alden, Edward 2005: "US calls for larger EU farm tariff cuts", *Financial Times*, Washington DC, 02 December.

Alvarez, Jose E. 2002: "The WTO as Linkage Machine", in *The American Journal of International Law*, Vol. 96, No. 1, pp. 146-158.

Anderson, Kym/ Yujiro Hayami 1986: *The Political Economy of Agricultural Protection*. Sydney, Australia: Allen & Unwin.

Anderson, Kym 1995: "Lobbying Incentives and the Pattern of Protection in Rich and Poor Countries", in *Economic Development and Cultural Change*, Vol. 43, No. 2, pp. 401-423.

Axelrod, Robert 1981: "The Emergence of Cooperation among Egoists", in *The American Political Science Review*, Vol. 75, No. 2, pp. 306-318.

Beattie, Alan 2005: "Farming subsidies could face legal threat", *Financial Times*, London, 30 November.

Benham, Frederick 1935: "Taxation and the Relative Prices of Factors of Production", in *Economia*, New Series, Vol. 2, No. 6, pp. 198-203.

– 1940: "The Terms of Trade", in *Economia,* New Series, Vol. 7, No 28, pp. 360-376.

Binswanger, Hans P./ Klaus Deininger 1997: „Explaining Agricultural and Agrarian Policies in Developing Countries", in *Journal of Economic Literature*, Vol. 35, No. 4, pp. 1958-2005

Buck, Tobias/ Guy de Jonquières 2004: "EU offers to scrap farm export subsidies", *Financial Times*, Brussels and Washington DC, 09 May.

Conybeare, John A. C. 1984: "Public Goods, Prisoners' Dilemmas and the International Political Economy", in *International Studies Quarterly*, Vol. 28, No. 1, pp. 5-22.

Copland, D. B. 1931: "A Neglected Phase of Tariff Controversy", in *The Quarterly Journal of Economics*, Vol. 45, No. 2, pp. 289-308.

Denny, Charlotte/ Larry Elliott 2003: "Developing nations keep up pressure", *Guardian*, Cancún, 12 September.

Elliott, Larry 2005: "Britain's stubbornness may help the world's poor", *Guardian*, 28 November.

Elliott, Larry/ Charlotte Denny 2003: "Breakdown means no end in sight to Doha Round", *Guardian*, Cancún, 16 September.

European Commission [no date]: The Common Agricultural Policy and the Lisbon Strategy.

(http://ec.europa.eu/agriculture/lisbon/index_en.htm, on 14.02.2007)

– [no date]: CAP Reform A Long-Term Perspective for Sustainable Agriculture.

(http://ec.europa.eu/agriculture/capreform/index_en.htm, on 14.02.2007)

European Communities 2004: *The Common Agricultural Policy Explained*: European Communities.

Financial Express, the 2005a: "EU stands ready to end farm export subsidies", 21 June.

– 2005b: "West draws flak for unfair farm trade practices", New Delhi, 07 September.

– 2006: "Bush's need for farm votes may have scuttled global trade deal", 28 July.

– 2007a: "Trade ministers agree to revive WTO", Davos, 28 January.

– 2007b: "EU must shun double standards: Bhagwati", New York, 17 February.

Foster, Nigel 2006: "Consolidated Version of the Treaty Establishing the European Community" (Conciliated Version in Accordance with the Treaty of Nice), in Nigel Foster (ed.): *Blackstone's EC Legislation 2006-2007* (17th Edition), London: Blackstone Press, pp. 1-103.

Frieden, Jeffrey A./ David A. Lake 2004 (eds.): *International Political Economy: Perspectives on Global Power and Wealth* (4th Edition), London, New York: Routledge.

Gallagher, Peter 2005: *The First Ten Years of the WTO (1995-2005)*, Cambridge: Cambridge University Press.

Gallagher, Peter et al (eds.) 2005: *Managing the Challenges of WTO Participation: 45 Cases Study Studies*, Cambridge: Cambridge University Press.

General Agreement on Tariffs and Trade 1994 (LT/UR/A-A1/1/GATT/2), 15 April.

Gerring, John 2001: *Social Science Methodology: A Critical Framework*, Cambridge: Cambridge University Press.

Goldstein, Judith 1989: "The Impact of Ideas on Trade Policy: The Origins of U.S. Agricultural and Manufacturing Policies", in *International Organization*, Vol. 43, No. 1, pp. 31-71.

Gourevitch, Peter 1978: "The Second Image Reversed: The International Sources of Domestic Politics", in *International Organization*, Vol. 32, No. 4, pp. 881-912.

Gowa, Joanne/ Edward D. Mansfield 1993: "Power Politics and International Trade", in *The American Political Science Review*, Vol. 87, No. 2, pp. 408-420.

Greider, William 2003: "Why the WTO Is Going Nowhere", *The Nation*, 04 September

Guardian, the 2005a: "Tony Blair's Mansion House speech: full text", 15 November.

- 2005b: "Report condemns 'illegal' EU agricultural subsidies", 30 November.

- 2005c: "Q&A: Britain's rebate from the EU", 02 December.

- 2005d: "It's not all bad news", 20 December.

- 2006: "Deep Concern over Doha suspension", 10 October.

Hardin, Garrett 1968: "The Tragedy of the Commons", in *Science*, Vol. 162, No. 3859, pp. 1243-1248.

Hardin, Russell 1971: "Collective Action as an Agreeable *n*-Prisoner's Dilemma", in *Behavioral Science*, Vol. 16, pp. 472-481.

Helm, Toby/ David Rennie 2005a: "Blair under Pressure to help Chirac win Constitution Vote", *Telegraph*, Brussels, 23 March.

- 2005b: "Chirac betrays Blair on Britain's rebate", *Telegraph*, Brussels, 24 March.

Henwood, Doug 2003: "Collapse in Cancún", *The Nation*, 10 October.

Hoeckman, Bernard/ Kym Anderson 2000: "Developing Country Agriculture and the New Trade Agenda", in *Economic Development and Cultural Change*, Vol. 49, No. 1, pp. 171-180.

Hollinger, Peggy 2005: "French business hits at farm lobby", *Financial Times*, Paris, 28 November.

IP/06/194: CAP Reform: EU Agriculture Ministers Adopt Groundbreaking Sugar Reform, Brussels, 20 February 2006.

IP/06/1591: Sugar Reform: Commissioner Fischer Boel urges further Efforts in Restructuring the EU Sugar Industry, Brussels, 21 November 2006.

IP/06/1708: Commission Proposes to allow Resale of Intervention Sugar for Export, Brussels, 07 December 2006.

IP/07/103: Commissioner Fischer Boel calls for Substantial Preventive Withdrawal from the Sugar Market to Avert Probable Surplus, Brussels, 29 January 2007.

IP/07/231: Preventive Sugar Withdrawal in 2007/ 08, Brussels, 23 February 2007.

Jawara, Fatouma/ Aileen Kwa 2004: *Behind the Scenes at the WTO: the Real World of International Trade*, London, New York: Zed Books.

Johnson, D. G. 1950: *Trade and Agriculture. A Study of Inconsistent Policies*, New York: John Wiley and Sons.

– 1973: *World Agriculture in Disarray*, New York: Saint Martin's Press (for) the Trade Policy Research Centre.

– 1991: *World Agriculture in Disarray* (2nd Edition), New York: Saint Martin's Press.

Jonquières, Guy de/ Edward Alden 2004: "Zoellick to call for all-out trade round effort", *Financial Times*, Washington DC, 09 May.

Josling, Tim 1993: "Multilateralism: A Constraint on Unilateralism and Regionalism in Agricultural Trade", in *American Journal of Agricultural Economics*, Vol. 75, No. 3, pp. 803-809.

Kahler, Miles 1992: "Multilateralism with Small and Large Numbers", in *International Organization*, Vol. 46, No.3, pp. 681-708.

Kahn, F. 2002: "EU Upbeat at the WTO Deal to Ease Access to Cheap Drugs for Poor", in Inter Press Service, 2 December. (www.aegis.com/news/ips/2002/IP021205.html)

Kaptur, Marcy 2006: "Saving Small Farmers", *The Nation*, 19 January.

Keohane, Robert O. 1986: "Reciprocity in International Relations", in *International Organization*, Vol. 40, No. 1, pp. 1-27.

– 1990: "Multilateralism: An Agenda for Research", In *International Organization*, Vol. 45, pp. 731-764.

Kim, HeeMin/ Dale L. Smith 1997: "Blocs or Rounds? An Analysis of Two Approaches to Trade Liberalization", in *Canadian Journal of Political Science/ Revue canadienne de science politique*, Vol. 30, No. 3, pp. 427-449.

Krugman, Paul R. 1987: "Is Free Trade Passé?" in *The Journal of Economic Perspectives*, Vol. 1, No. 2, Papers and Proceedings of the Hundred and Fifth Annual Meeting of the American Economic association, pp. 131-144.

– 1993: "The Narrow and Broad Arguments for Free Trade", in *The American Economic Review* Vol. 83, No. 2, Paper and Proceedings of the Hundred and Fifth Annual Meeting of the American Economic Association, pp. 362-366.

Krugman, Paul R./ Obsfeld, Maurice 2000: *International Economics: Theory and Policy* (5th Edition), New York: Addison-Wesley.

Legro, Jeffrey W. 1996: "Culture and Preferences in the International Cooperation Two-Step", in *The American Political Science Review*, Vol. 90, No. 1, pp. 118-137.

Lida, Keisuke 1993: "When and How Do Domestic Constraints Matter? Two-Level Games with Uncertainty", in *The Journal of Conflict Resolution*, Vol. 37, No.3, pp. 403-426.

Lukas, Aaron/ Marci Hilt 2003a: "Zoellick to Meet with Caribbean Trade Ministers", USTR Press release, Washington DC, 30 June.

– 2003b: "Zoellick/ Veneman statement on EU CAP Policy", USTR Press release, 26 June.

Mahler, Vincent A. 1991: "Domestic & International Sources of Trade Policy: The Case of Agriculture in the European Community & the United States", in *Polity*, Vol. 24, No. 1, pp. 27-47.

Margaronis, Maria 1999: "The Politics of Food", in *The Nation*, 9 December.

Mathiason, Nick 2003: "Subsidies sow seeds of ruin", *Guardian,* Cancún, 07 September.

Martin, Lisa L. 1992: "Interests, Power, and Multilateralism", in *International Organization*, Vol. 46, No. 4, pp. 765-792.

Mayer, Frederick W. 1992: "Managing Domestic Differences in International Negotiations: The Strategic Use of Internal Side-Payments", in *International Organization*, Vol. 46, No. 4, pp. 793-818.

McCalla, Alex F. 1993: "Agricultural Trade Liberalization: The Ever-Elusive Grail", in *American Journal of Agricultural Economics*, Vol. 75, No. 5, Proceedings Issue, pp. 1102-1112.

Mehta, Pradeep S. 2001: "Agriculture: Tough to quantify benefits now", *The Financial Express*, 25 December.

– 2005: "Agriculture negotiations hold the key to success", *The Financial Express*, 14 December.

Mills, Richard 2002: "USTR notifies Congress Administration Intends to Initiate Free Trade Negotiations with Sub-Saharan Nations", USTR Press release, Washington DC, 05 November.

Mo, Jongryn 1994: "The Logic of Two-Level Games with Endogenous Domestic Coalitions", in *The Journal of Conflict Resolution*, Vol. 38, No. 3, pp. 402-422.

Moravcsik, Andrew 1997: "Taking Preferences Seriously: A Liberal Theory of International Politics", *International Organization*, Vol. 51, No. 4, pp. 513-553.

Mulholland, Hélène 2006: "Cameron to call for EU reform", *Guardian*, 07 December.

Oatley, Thomas 2004: *International Political Economy: Interests and Institutions in the Global Economy*, New York: Pearson Longman.

OECD 2005: *Preferential Trading Arrangements in Agricultural and Food Markets: The Cases of the European Union and the United States*, Paris: OECD

Olson, Mancur 1968: *The Logic of Collective Action*, New York: Schocken.

Osborn, Andrew 2003: "Brussels offers three ways to start CAP reform", *Guardian*, Brussels, 24 September.

Osborn, Andrew/ Larry Elliott 2003: "EU farm chief slams poor nations' demands", *Guardian*, Brussels, 05 September.

Oxfam 2002a: *Europe's Double Standards: How the EU should reform its Trade Policies with the Developing World* (Oxfam Briefing Paper No. 22): Oxfam International.

– 2002b: *Cultivating Poverty: The Impact of US Cotton Subsidies on Africa* (Oxfam Briefing Paper No. 30): Oxfam International.

– 2002c: *Boxing Match in Agricultural Trade: Will WTO Negotiations knock out the World's Poorest Farmers* (Oxfam Briefing Paper No. 32): Oxfam International.

– 2002d: *Rigged Rules and Double Standards: Trade, Globalization, and the Fight against Poverty*: Oxfam Great Britain.

– 2004a: *Dumping on the World: How EU Sugar Policies Hurt Poor Countries* (Oxfam Briefing Paper No. 61): Oxfam International.

– 2004b: *Dumping: the Beginning of the End? Implications of the Ruling in the Brazil/ US Cotton Dispute* (Oxfam Briefing Paper No. 64): Oxfam International.

– 2004c: *An End to EU Sugar Dumping? Implications of the Interim WTO Panel Ruling in the Dispute against EU Sugar Policies brought by Brazil, Thailand, and Australia* (Oxfam Briefing Note): Oxfam International.

Paarlberg, R. L. 1988: *Fixing Farm Trade: Policy Options for the United States*, Cambridge, MA: Ballinger.

– 1989: "The Political Economy of American Agricultural Policy: Three Approaches", in American Journal of Agricultural Economics, Vol. 71, No. 5, Proceedings Issue, pp. 1157-1164.

– 1997: "Agricultural Policy Reform and the Uruguay Round: Synergic Linkage in a Two-Level Game? In *International Organization*, Vol. 51, No. 3, pp. 413-444.

Pahre, Robert 1994: "Multilateral Cooperation in an Iterated Prisoner's Dilemma", in *The Journal of Conflict Resolution*, Vol. 38, No. 2, Arms, Alliances, and Cooperation: Formal Models and Empirical Tests, pp. 326-352.

Patterson, Lee Ann 1997: "Agricultural Policy Reform in the European Community: A Three-Level Game Analysis", in *International Organization*, Vol. 51, No. 1, pp. 135-165.

Putnam, Robert D. 1988: "Diplomacy and Domestic Politics: The Logic of Two-Level Games", in *International Organization*, Vol. 42, No. 3, pp. 427-460.

Rahman, Bayan/ Frances Williams 2003: "Sides line up to contest farm reform", *Financial Times*, Tokyo and Geneva, 14 February.

Ravenhill, John (ed.) 2005: *Global political Economy*, Oxford, New York: Oxford University Press.

Rennie, David 2005a: "EU Plot to grab Britain's Rebate", *Telegraph*, Luxembourg, 08 June.

– 2005b: "Eurocrats threaten to obstruct Blair's Plans", *Telegraph*, Brussels, 21 June.

Rennie, David/ Toby Helm 2005a: "Blair under Pressure to Help Chirac win Constitution Vote", *Telegraph*, 23 March.

– 2005b: “Chirac betrays Blair on Britain’s rebate”, *Telegraph*, 24 March.

Reuters 2007a: “EU urges US to seize opportunity for Doha deal”, Press release, 05 January.

– 2007b: “Congress, poised to overhaul farm bill, eyes Doha”, Press release, 30 January.

– 2007c: “US Democrats urge action vs. ‘Big 3’ trade partners”, Press release, 13 February.

Rivoli, Pietra 2005: *The Travels of T-Shirt in the Global Economy: An Economist Examines the Markets, and Politics of World Trade*, Wiley: John Wiley & Sons, Inc.

Ruggie, John Gerard 1982: “International Regimes, Transactions, and Change: Embedded Liberalism in the Postwar Economic Order”, in *International Organization*, Vol. 36, No. 2, pp. 379-415.

– 1992: “Multilateralism: the Anatomy of an Institution”, in *International Organization*, Vol. 46, No. 3, pp. 561-598.

Runge, C. Ford/ Harald von Witze 1990: “European Community Enlargement and Institutional Choice in the Common Agricultural Policy”, in *American Journal of Political Science*, Vol. 34, No. 1, pp. 254-268.

Samuelson, Paul A. 1939: “The Gains from International Trade”, in *The Canadian Journal of Economics and Political Science/ Revue canadienne d´Economique et de Science Politique*, Vol. 5, No. 2, pp. 195-205.

– 1948: “International Trade and the Equalization of Factor Prices”, in *The Economic Journal*, Vol. 58, No. 230, pp. 163-184.

Sharma, Ashok B. 2005: “US, EU should learn from WTO body’s rulings on cotton, sugar”, *The Financial Express*, 14 March.

Schott, Jeffrey J. 1994: *The Uruguay Round: An Assessment*, Washington, DC: Institute for International Economics.

Smith, Adam 1776/ 1976: *An Inquiry into the Nature and Causes of the Wealth of Nations*. Oxford: Oxford University Press.

Snidal, Duncan 1985: "Coordination versus Prisoners' Dilemma: Implications for International Cooperation and Regimes", in *The American Political Science Review*, Vol. 79, No. 4, pp. 923-942.

SPEECH/06/622: Mariann Fischer Boel, Member of the European Commission Responsible for Agriculture and Rural Development: 'The CAP in the European Scenario', International Forum on Agriculture and Food, Press Release, Cernobbio, Italy, 20 October 2006.

SPEECH/07/72: Mariann Fischer Boel, Member of the European Commission Responsible for Agriculture and Rural Development: 'EU Agriculture in a Globalised World', Event Hosted by the Carnegie Endowment for International Peace, Press Release, Washington, 9 February 2007.

Stolper, Wolfgang F./ Paul A. Samuelson 1941: "Protection and Real Wages", in *The Review of Economics Studies*, Vol. 9, No. 1, pp. 58-73.

Tyers, R./ K. Anderson 1992: *Disarray in World Food Markets: A Quantitative Assessment*, Cambridge, NY: Cambridge University Press.

USDA 2003a: WTO: Uruguay Round Agreement on Agriculture: Export Subsidies.

(http://www.ers.usda.gov/briefing/wto/exptsubs.htm, on 26.02.2007)

– 2003b: WTO: Uruguay Round Agreement on Agriculture: Tariffs and Market Access.

(http://www.ers.usda.gove/briefing/wto/tariffsmktac.htm, on 26.02.2007)

– 2004: WTO: Uruguay Round Agreement on Agriculture: Domestic Support.

(http://www.ers.usda.gov/briefing/wto/domsupport.htm, on 26.02.2007)

USTR 2004: "Trade with Sub-Saharan Africa: AGOA is the Cornerstone of Success", Press release, 25 June.

- 2005a: "Acting USTR Allgeier to Attend Informal Meeting of Trade Ministers, in Kenya, March 3-4", Press release, 28 February.

- 2005b: "US Offers Bold Plan on Agriculture to Jumpstart Doha Round", Press release, 10 October.

- 2005c: "US Announces Launch of West African Cotton Improvement Program", Press release, 10 November.

- 2005d: "USTR Announces Additional Allocation of Sugar Imports for African and Caribbean Countries", Press release, 09 December.

Van den Berg, Hendrik 2004: *International Economics*, New York: McGraw Hill/Irwin.

Van Evera, Stephan 1997: *Guide to Methods for Students of Political Science*, Ithaca, NY: Cornell University Press.

Warley, T. K. 1989: "Agriculture in the GATT: A Historical Perspective", in *Agriculture in the Uruguay Round of GATT Negotiations: Implications for Canada's and Ontario's Agrifood Systems*, Guelph, Ontario: University of Guelph.

World Trade Organization 2002: *International Trade Statistics*. Geneva: World Trade Organization.

- 2005: *Understanding the WTO*. Geneva: World Trade Organization.

WT/L/579: Text of the 'July Package' – the General Council post-Cancún Decision, 2 August 2004.

WT/MIN(01)/DEC/1: Doha Ministerial Declaration, 20 November 2001.

*ibidem*-Verlag
Melchiorstr. 15
D-70439 Stuttgart

info@ibidem-verlag.de

www.ibidem-verlag.de
www.edition-noema.de
www.autorenbetreuung.de

Zeitfracht Medien GmbH
Ferdinand-Jühlke-Straße 7
99095 Erfurt, Deutschland
produktsicherheit@kolibri360.de